D0295680

THE ❧ ❧
ERSKINES
EBENEZER
AND RALPH

FAMOUS SCOTS SERIES

The following Volumes are now ready:—

THE ERSKINES

BY A R MacEWEN

FAMOUS ·SCOTS· ·SERIES·

PUBLISHED BY
OLIPHANT ANDERSON
& FERRIER·EDINBVRGH
AND LONDON

The designs and ornaments of this volume are by Mr Joseph Brown, and the printing from the press of Messrs Turnbull & Spears, Edinburgh.

April 1900

TO

M. J. M.

CONTENTS

CHAPTER I

PREFACE

THE biographies of the Erskines by the Rev. Donald Fraser, published in 1831 and 1833, present their personal character with great fulness. Mr Fraser had access to documents not now available—a diary kept by Ebenezer from 1707 till 1722, a diary kept by Ralph from 1731 till 1739, and other manuscripts in shorthand. Admirably as he portrayed their inner life, his narrative is bare and has failed to interest those to whom the events of the Secession are not familiar.

As to the historical position and influence of the Erskines, many writers have blundered by following implicitly M'Kerrow's *History of the Secession Church*. M'Kerrow was a scrupulously careful writer, but his reluctance to reopen recently healed wounds made him silent at points where historical accuracy required frankness. Principal Harper's *Memoir of Ebenezer Erskine*, and Dr John Brown's *Memoir of Fisher*, show less reserve, and are marked as might be expected by breadth and clearness. If even Harper and Brown touch overlightly upon the faults of the 'Secession Fathers,' Established Church writers on the other hand have not recognised their merits. It ought to be possible now to write without bias. Archbishop Eyre has kindly guided me to the authorities accepted by the Roman Catholic Church. Among the Church historians of Scotland, Mr George Grub is unrivalled in patient accuracy, and Principal Lee in fairness and research.

In order to reach the realities, one must turn to the writings of the Erskines and compare these with contemporary literature. With regard to the latter, the most important information is contained in rare pamphlets, many of which have been carefully studied. Of Erskine letters and Erskine reminiscences, which have appeared at intervals in denominational magazines, a cautious use has been made. Boston's *Memoirs*, Morren's *Annals of the Assembly*, Chambers' *Domestic Annals of Scotland*, Tait's *Border Church Life*, Ferrier's *Life of Wilson*, M'Kelvie's *Annals and Statistics* and Moncrieff's *Life of Dr John Erskine*, have been consulted at many points. In more recent literature recognition is due to Mr E. E. Scott's *Erskine-Halcro Genealogy*; Principal Story's *William Carstares*; Dr Mitchell's St Giles' *Lecture on the Erskines*; Mr Butler's *Wesley and Whitefield in Scotland*; Mr G. H. Morrison's *Introduction* to Boston's Memoirs; and, above all, Dr John Ker's appreciation of the Erskines in *Scottish Nationality*. Mr H. G. Graham in his *Social Life of Scotland* gives some interesting views of the eighteenth century; but his humorous account of the Erskines will not bear scrutiny.

Mr John Mair, Librarian of the United Presbyterian Church, has been helpful in guiding me to valuable documents. Mr J. R. Anderson and the Rev. John Young have kindly read the proofs and made many suggestions.

A. R. M.

GLASGOW, *April* 1900.

THE ERSKINES

CHAPTER I

PRELIMINARY

AT the beginning of the eighteenth century the Church life of Scotland was in transition and presented many strange contrasts. In some parts of the country these arose from conflict between Presbyterianism, Episcopacy and Roman Catholicism, and were coloured by racial and political differences; but in central and southern Scotland, with which alone the following narrative is concerned, the Reformed Church and Hanoverian sympathies prevailed almost exclusively. Of Roman Catholics, who numbered in all Scotland about fourteen thousand, only a hundred and sixty were in 1705 resident in Edinburgh, five at Leith, twelve at Glasgow, twenty at Perth. The Episcopal Church as a separate corporation scarcely existed. From 1689 till 1712 liturgical worship was illegal, and even after the Act of Toleration it was introduced only in some private chapels and in a few towns where there were resident Englishmen. In 1726 there was not a single diocesan bishop in Scotland. Those Episcopalians who in the north retained possession of parish churches, rarely sent representatives to the General Assembly, and took little concern in the general life of the Church. The desire of William of Orange to create a fusion of Episcopacy with Presbyterianism had come to nothing. Queen Anne's attempt to favour the Scottish Episcopalians was baffled by their adherence to the Pretender. Their political action, especially in the

Rebellion of 1715, excluded them from all districts which were loyal to the House of Hanover. To the Scotsmen about whom we have to speak, Episcopalians were 'prelatists' and 'malignants,' who must be kept at a distance, with disregard of personal ties, as the opponents of the Reformed Church and of the reigning dynasty.

It is true that, even in the lowlands, the Established Church included among its ministers many who had been trained and ordained as Episcopalians. In 1710 there were about sixty south of the Tay. In some cases those men occupied the parish manses and preached in the parish churches to empty pews, while the parishioners frequented and supported the ministry of Presbyterians, being as it were Established Church dissenters. In other cases the irregularity was still more glaring. At Dunfermline, for instance, which was a collegiate charge, an Episcopalian conducted the service in the parish church on Sunday mornings, and a Presbyterian on Sunday afternoons. But those anomalies rapidly disappeared. Within thirty years of the Revolution the race of Episcopalian parish ministers had almost died out. Even while they lived they had little influence. Episcopalian historians have perhaps been too sweeping and severe in denunciation of their personal character; but at their best they were place-holders, who had acknowledged Presbyterianism to be 'the only government of the Church in this land,' in order to retain their manses and their stipends, and as such they were everywhere discounted or ignored. There is no foundation for the statement frequently made by controversialists, both Roman Catholic and Presbyterian, that they swayed the counsels of the Church. Nor had they any effect upon the religion of their parishioners, who adhered to Presbyterian worship and doctrine, cherished proud recollections of the Covenanting days, and spoke with gratitude of the 'glorious Revolution.' The only traces they left when they died were in the disorder of church fabrics and of parochial organisation.

Undoubtedly there was a difference between localities. In some districts, especially south-east of Edinburgh, the landlords had established a species of serfdom, with an accompanying social degradation in which independent church life was impossible. In the south-west and south, on the other hand, where the Cameronians had gained sway, a spirit of stubborn and suspicious isolation prevailed, and asserted itself in condemnation of the Revolution Settlement as not thorough in its dealings with Episcopacy. When Boston settled at Ettrick he found that every hamlet had its separatists. But those extremes were local and exceptional. Novelists and essayists in search of the picturesque have greatly exaggerated their importance. In parish after parish and town after town, indeed in county after county, the Established Church, the Church of the Revolution, was the church and the only church of the people. In that dearth of literary, artistic, and intellectual production which characterised the period, it supplied them with their mental as well as their spiritual food. The parish church was their only meeting-place. The pulpit was their only source of information regarding national affairs. Presbyteries and Sessions gave them their laws of living, laws which affected them more than the legislation of the Scots Estates or the British Parliament. Presbyterianism was undivided and undisputed in its rule.

The religious life of the people, so far as it was spiritual and free, depended largely upon the Sacrament of the Lord's Supper, the observance of which was a distinctive feature of eighteenth century Presbyterianism. Individual congregations observed the Sacrament rarely, often with intervals of years. In the parish of Liddesdale, for instance, when the minister persuaded his elders to revive the observance, it was discovered that there were no

Communion vessels. Yet it is only ignorance which has led ecclesiastical writers to the idea that in such parishes there was no recognition of Sacramental grace. The observance was not a parochial one. When a celebration was intimated in any one parish, hundreds and often thousands of people poured into it from the neighbouring parishes and remained for three, four, or five days, listening from morning till night to a series of sermons which culminated in the sacred rite. There were none of the abuses of this usage which crept in afterwards, and which Burns has branded in his description of Holy Fairs. It was the more serious and earnest of the people who frequented such assemblies. Young men when preparing for ordination would spend many weeks in attending Sacraments, riding or walking across country from one parish to another. When the faithful preachers of the day condemned those who 'ran from Sacrament to Sacrament,' their condemnation rested upon the strain which the practice laid upon religious emotion. Their language, which was always respectful and kindly, might be applied with but slight modification to the modern practice of attending conferences, congresses and retreats.

Those celebrations had a direct bearing upon the history of the Church. In every district they created a bond between the religiously disposed, who became acquainted with one another and exchanged views upon church affairs, gaining in this way an independence of parish limits and some width of outlook. They also gave great influence to the ministers who were most in request on such occasions, for the sermons were as a rule neither rhetorical displays nor appeals to sentiment, but careful expositions of Bible doctrine, with measured references to the questions which were before the Church of the day.

This non-parochial and non-ecclesiastical force was strengthened and made permanent by an agency which survived from the days of the Covenant. The country was permeated by 'Societies,' which met fortnightly or monthly for prayer, and which were mainly composed of the men who frequented Sacraments. Neighbouring Societies met once or twice a year for conference, and corresponded with one another, each group of Societies being termed a Correspondence. While this institution obviously contained elements in which dissent might find a home, it was in the first instance religious rather than controversial. Far from representing any antagonism to the Church, it gave a rallying ground to those who, within the Church, were specially attached to orthodox beliefs and to the principles of the Reformation. It was only when a parish minister was careless or inefficient that the Societies ceased to support him. Usually the leading spirit was an elder of the Church, and the parish minister gave the Society his countenance.

The Church of Scotland, however, as a recognised corporation, was very slightly influenced by any of those tides of religious life. Its policy and polity were controlled by the General Assembly, which, though nominally a representative court, did not adequately represent the popular religion, and was subject to outside influences. At the Revolution the Assembly had taken shape in accordance with the policy of Principal Carstares, to whose rare abilities the Revolution Settlement had been largely due. The attempts of the survivors of the Covenanters to adapt the Settlement to their exclusive views were opposed by the determination of William that there should be neither persecution nor banning of Episcopalians, and Carstares had trained the Assembly to accept the situation and to recognise within certain limits the influence of King and Court. Before 1707, according to the biographers of Carstares, the ascendancy of the Moderate party was established. Yet the word Moderate had not then the sense which it gained in the middle of the eighteenth century. As yet there was no doctrinal laxity except in embryo, nor any justification for calling the party of Carstares secular, at least by way of reproach. It could scarcely indeed be styled liberal. Carstares himself headed deputations sent by the Assembly to London, to protest against toleration and against other infringements upon rigid and orthodox Presbyterianism. In the way of protest he went as far as he deemed possible and safe. His policy was to object, to contend, to resist, and then, when resistance failed, to concede, as though the point conceded had not been vital. His party, as it first came to rule the Assembly, may be best designated the party of concession. Its attitude is well illustrated by a passage of arms between two of the recognised wits of the House of Commons. When the Act of Union was under discussion, Sir John Packington urged that the two kingdoms could not unite, since each of them held that its Church was established by divine right. To this Colonel Mordaunt responded that divine right meant ' God's permission,' and that since God had permitted Episcopacy to prevail in England and Presbyterianism to prevail in Scotland, the divine right of the one in no way detracted from the divine right of the other. In this humorous equivocation Carstares persuaded his party to acquiesce seriously. Dr Calamy, a shrewd observer, who visited the Assembly in 1709, reported that of many members of the Court with whom he conversed, not one contended for the divine right of Presbytery. In the very next year the Rev. John Anderson, responding to a challenge from Robert Calder, one of the rabbled curates, set himself to show the scriptural authority of Presbyterianism, and so began a controversy by which the Church generally was for five years profoundly stirred. Yet the Assembly had little interest in the controversy. Claiming no sanction except expediency for its constitution, offices, and methods, it was all but ready to concede what is distinctive of Presbyterianism with few qualms of conscience and a slight sense of loss.

As long as Carstares lived, his party acted prudently, consistently and successfully. If he had had a successor of equal powers, the history of the Church of Scotland might have been completely different, and the road by which the Erskines reached a place among Famous Scots might never have been opened. But after his death, in 1715, the party lost its bearings through want of brain power. No competent leader appeared till 1751, when Robertson the historian inaugurated a new régime. For thirty-five years the majority were headed by ecclesiastics of second-rate ability, under whose guidance they blundered and floundered. From year to year they shifted their attitude without valid reason. On one important question after another they reversed their decisions in obedience to popular clamour, and destroyed their own workmanship, only to piece its fragments together when the destruction proved to be useless. Even those who commend their general policy deplore their vacillation and inconsistency, while their severest judges recognise that, if they had been clear in their purpose and firm in their action, their cause might have had complete success.

One important result of this want of leadership was that power was thrown into the hands of the able politicians who were lay members of Assembly, and of the lawyers who appeared as counsel in debated cases. Such men as Archibald, Earl of Ilay, and Erskine of Grange, served on every important Committee, and led in most important discussions. Under guides of that type, religion and the Church were in obvious peril. In cases of libel, the Assembly sometimes heard as many as five or six professional advocates on each side. It was not cowardice that made the ordinary member of Assembly slow to raise his voice after the protagonists of Parliament House had been heard. It came to be regarded indeed as a breach of etiquette if anyone spoke except at the special request of the Moderator. Country elders of the middle class, who now form so powerful an element in the Assemblies, were never heard. The church annals show that almost all the laymen appointed to deal with critical affairs were lawyers, noblemen, or wealthy landlords resident in Edinburgh. So it came about that the Assembly was frequently unacquainted with the views which prevailed throughout the country, and that the Assembly majority came into collision with Synods and Presbyteries, which, as local courts, knew the mind of the people in their localities.

With regard to those who formed the minority in the Assembly, all that need be said at this stage is that their position may be defined by contrast. They would, if they could, have insisted on the divine right of Presbytery, and they steadily objected to every departure from Reformation principles. At the beginning of the century they had neither a name nor a policy. Although they were the precursors of the evangelicals, they had as yet no distinctive doctrines. They were intensely national, and their ideal was a Covenanted nation. While Hanoverian in their sympathies, they valued the Revolution Settlement only so far as it restored the earlier settlements of the seventeenth century and the original establishment of the Reformed religion. They were restive under Court influence, and disposed to shut their eyes to the fact that Episcopacy was established in England, as an unpleasant incident which they declined to take into consideration. Their watchword was that of their fathers—Christ's Crown and Covenant; but they had not measured what that watchword would soon mean for Scotsmen.

In the twenty years that followed the Revolution several individuals, more or less identified with this party, had left the Church and gathered adherents who became known by their names, as M'Millanites, Hepburnites, Taylorites, etc.; but none of these had power of growth or even cohesiveness. They had neither principle nor policy, except to deplore the disappearance of a past which had existed only for a few years, after the Glasgow Assembly of 1638. Like the Cameronians, who remained outside the Revolution Church, they were merely protesters, and in religious affairs those who merely protest are always barren. With the lives of their founders the ecclesiastical existence of those bodies ended.

The minority in the Assembly had a future in store for it in two directions. Within the Established Church it existed on sufferance for a century, through the pious local ministrations of men who were silent in the Church Courts, and thereafter broke out into a fulness of life which has given vitality to the Established Church during the century now drawing to a close. But it had another channel of existence, by which also it reached the nineteenth century. It became a separate, living body and a visible element in the life of the nation, when it gained principles and leaders. Its principles were two-fold— the free presentation of the Gospel, and the equal rights of Christian men. Its leaders were the Erskines.

In a volume of this size no attempt can be made to present pictorially the social condition of the times. Lord Rosebery recently pointed out, with great accuracy, that the inner history of Scotland in the eighteenth century has not yet been told, and that there is no adequate record of the multiform movements through which the country gathered herself together for the important part she was destined to play in the life of the British Empire. The materials for such a record can be obtained only by copious and discreet biography, exhibiting the normal thoughts and habits of the people. The historian must not be satisfied with quoting cases of discipline brought before kirk-sessions, and criminal cases quoted in lawbooks. The structure of dwelling-houses, the food men eat, the clothes they wear, and other details of domestic habits have some interest and significance; but they do not constitute history. Two centuries ago Scotland was a poor country; but poverty does not imply meagreness or meanness. The life of the Erskines was in all essentials marked by moral dignity, by courtesy of manners, and by culture of thought and feeling. If their intimate journals show no trace of social inferiority or domestic ugliness, and might have been written amidst the refined comforts of academic serenity, it is only an illustration of the truth that it is by inward realities that character is shaped and conduct is determined.

CHAPTER II

BIRTH AND TRAINING

THE Erskines were sons of the Rev. Henry Erskine,[1] minister of Chirnside, by his second wife Margaret Halcro of Orkney. Ebenezer was born at Dryburgh on June 22, 1680, and Ralph at Monilaws, in Northumberland, on March 15, 1685.

They had the best blood of Scotland in their veins. Their father was one of the Erskines of Shielfield, in Roxburghshire, direct descendants of Robert, third Lord Erskine, who died at Flodden. The Erskine clan was widespread, and its branches diverged in politics and religion. In 1557 Erskine of Dun subscribed the Godly Band, becoming one of the Lords of the Congregation, and in 1639 Lord Erskine was the first elder to take the Covenant. One branch, the Balgownie branch, was tenaciously Roman Catholic. In another, to which the earldom of Mar belonged, there was a tulchan archbishop of Glasgow. But amidst such divergences, the clan in antique spirit recognised its kinship cordially. The Countess of Mar acted as Ebenezer's godmother. James Erskine of Grange, that picturesque but unattractive religious phenomenon, served Ralph as groomsman; and in other more important respects the career of both brothers was affected by their descent.

The Erskines had another strain in their blood, less

[1] The name was variously written—Iriskyn, Harskyne and Areskine. Both brothers frequently signed Areskine, and the name is usually so written in Assembly and Presbytery records.

aristocratic but quite as interesting. In 1559 the first Erskine of Shielfield married Elizabeth Haliburton, niece of the Thomas Haliburton to whom Sir Walter Scott traced his descent. In Dryburgh Abbey Sir Walter lies beside men who were not only his ancestors but ancestors of the Erskines. He was probably unaware of the connection, which has only lately been discovered. Do we owe Jeanie Deans, the Seceder's daughter, and the nobility of her quiet heroism, to some deep-lying sympathy of race?

Margaret Halcro had a pedigree more than equal to her husband's, being descended from an ancient Orkney family. A legend that one of her direct ancestors was a certain Prince Halcro of Norway has failed to stand historical scrutiny. It has been proved that Prince Halcro was a myth; but she had Scottish royalty in her ancestry, as a grand-daughter of Bernard Stewart, one of the Lennox Darnley Stewarts of Barscube. She was also an Erskine. Her grandmother, Helen Erskine of Dun, was banished from Scotland in 1620 for implication in a crime committed by her brother; but the family connection was maintained. It was when visiting her kinswoman, the Countess of Mar, that Margaret won the affections of her more distant kinsman Henry Erskine.

Henry Erskine, who was born at Dryburgh in 1624, was ordained as Presbyterian minister of Cornhill, a Northumberland village two miles from the Tweed, about the middle of the seventeenth century. Presbyterianism was then in power on both sides of the river, with its new Confession of Faith sanctioned by Parliament, and the early years of Erskine's ministry were spent in peaceful parochial labours. In 1662 he was one of the two thousand ministers who were ejected from their parishes by the Act of Uniformity. Several offers of comfortable livings were made to him on condition of his conforming to Episcopacy, but he resolutely rejected them. He made a journey to London in the hope of recovering arrears of his stipend which, for some unknown reason, had not been paid, and legendary incidents of his journey show that he was a brave and devoted minister who used every opportunity of preaching the gospel. Otherwise, however, the journey was unsuccessful, and in 1663 he settled at Dryburgh, where his brother, the laird of Shielfield, furnished him with a house. His intention was to act as the minister of those who refused to conform, but the intention was thwarted by the Act of 1663, which forbade ejected ministers to exercise their gifts. The re-establishment of the Court of High Commission in 1664 made the Act a grim reality. Yet Erskine disregarded it and preached in his own house and in the fields, pursuing his favourite study of church history when his preaching was interrupted. It was probably through the influence of his titled relatives that he had some freedom for this irregular ministry, but their help did not suffice to keep him out of poverty. By his first wife, who lived till 1670, he had eight children, and the household was repeatedly on the verge of starvation. Marvellous deliverances, through the timely assistance of kindly neighbours, were treasured episodes in the domestic history, and coloured the religion of the family. It was not till after the assassination of Sharp and the Battle of Bothwell Bridge that the stroke of direct persecution fell upon them. That their poverty was not continuous, may be inferred from the upbringing of the children, one of whom became rector of Knaresdale in Northumberland, while another entered good society in Edinburgh as the wife of an eminent surgeon. Erskine's first wife died, as we have seen, in 1670, and four years later he married Margaret Halcro, whose wedded life was to be attended by trials harder than poverty. The certificate which she brought from her home in Orkney gives interesting proof that church sessions were as careful censors of the aristocracy as of the poor, and that it was not, as recent writers have suggested, a jealous regard for the poor-box that prompted their carefulness :—

'At the Kirk of Evie, May 27, 1666.

' To all and sundry into whose hands these presents shall come, be it known that the bearer hereof, Margaret Halcro, daughter of the deceased Hugh Halcro in the Isle of Weir, and Margaret Stewart his spouse, hath lived in the Parish of Evie from her infancy in good fame and report, is a discreet, godly young woman, and to our certain knowledge free from all scandal, reproach, or blame. As also that she is descended by her father of the house of Halcro, which is a very ancient and honourable family in the Orkneys, the noble and potent Earl of Early, and the lairds of Dun in Angus, and by her mother of the lairds of Barscube, in Galloway. In witness thereof, we, the minister and clerk, have subscribed these presents at Evie, day, year, month of God, and place aforesaid, and give way to all the noblemen, gentlemen, and ministers to do the same.'—*Sic Subscribitur.*

Ebenezer was the third child of this marriage. He was born on a critical day, the very day on which Cameron and Cargill posted on Sanquhar market-cross the Declaration in which they disowned Charles Stuart, because of his tyranny and his breaches of the Covenant. In his early infancy persecution broke out into its last and most furious blaze, from which neither birth nor influence could give shelter. In 1682 Henry Erskine was arrested for 'withdrawing from ordinances, keeping conventicles, and being guilty of disorderly baptisms since the Indemnity Act of 1679.' On May 12th he was examined before the Committee of Privy Council by Sir George Mackenzie, who, after long cross-questioning, asked him if he would give a bond to preach no more at conventicles. Erskine replied : ' My Lord, I have my commission from Christ, and, though I were within an hour of my death, I durst not lay it down at the feet of any mortal man.' The application of the thumbscrew having failed to secure submission, the case was adjourned for three weeks, when he was re-examined by the Lord Chancellor Gordon. No witnesses were produced and he declined to give evidence against himself, but he was declared guilty and sentenced to imprisonment on the Bass Rock. His health was at this time broken through ague, and the Council complied with a petition that exile might be substituted for imprisonment, a nephew becoming surety in a bond of 5000 merks that he would not return to Scotland. For the next two years he lived at a village near Carlisle, his family remaining at Dryburgh. In 1684 he found a home for them at Monilaws, a hamlet within two miles of his former parish, and there, in 1685, Ralph was born. Two months later he was again arrested and taken to Newcastle, where he all but died in prison through the harshness of his jailors; but his patience and piety awakened sympathy and secured his liberation. Returning to Monilaws, he remained there for two years, preaching as occasion presented itself. On the Declaration of Toleration in 1687 he accepted a call to minister to the Presbyterians of the Scottish parish of Whitsome, a few miles west of Berwick, in a meeting-house at the hamlet of Rivelaw. The most notable incident of his Whitsome ministry was the conversion of Thomas Boston, the author of *The Fourfold State*. Boston, when aged 11, was taken across the hills by his father to the Rivelaw meeting-house, and there was 'brought under exercise about his soul's state, and led to pray in earnest.' Thereafter for some years he steadily attended Erskine's ministry, finding that he was more than repaid for the long trudge by 'the benefit of the word, which always came with power.'

After the Revolution the adjacent parish of Chirnside fell vacant, and Erskine, learning that his flock was willing to remove to the parish church, accepted a call to the vacancy. Though now an elderly man, he set himself eagerly to rouse the slumbering religion of the parishioners and to reorganise the Presbytery, of which he at once became the leading member. After an eight years' ministry, the fragrance of which lingered in the neighbourhood for several generations, he passed away on August 10, 1696. His wife and five of his children, including Ebenezer and Ralph, surrounded his deathbed, and from all of them, in the language of his school, he 'took engagements' to personal religion. Twenty years afterwards Ralph recalled gratefully 'the Lord's drawing out of his heart towards Him at his father's death.'

If Ralph's heart was drawn out towards God, the reflections of Ebenezer, who was by this time a student at Edinburgh University, must have been full of questioning. His dying father had been a consistent and loyal Presbyterian, but his consistency and loyalty had brought him, in the course of his changeful life, into a strange variety of relations to the civil powers. Ordained at a time when the Church dominated the State, he had been ejected from the Church of England, and persecuted in Scotland, by the civil powers, because he adhered to his Church principles. Thereafter the State, while itself Episcopalian, had allowed him to exercise a Presbyterian ministry, and finally he had been brought into the ministry of the Church of Scotland, because the State had returned to Presbyterianism. The ideas to which such a career gave birth in Ebenezer's mind were as yet undeveloped, but they were destined to grow.

How Henry Erskine had maintained and educated his family during his years of exile, it is impossible to say. Latterly, he seems to have been entirely dependent upon his stipend, for his death plunged the household into difficulties. The Privy Council records of 1697 preserve a successful petition from his widow for 'the stipend of the by-past half-year during which the parish had been vacant, she being left in a verie low and mean condition, with four fatherless children no way provided for, and other burdensome circumstances under which she was heavily pressed.' Yet she emerged from her low and mean condition, continued the education of the younger children, and sent Ebenezer back to Edinburgh to complete his preparation for the ministry.

The University was in disorder, having just been 'purged' of its Episcopalian professors. Students were taught Greek, Ethics, Pneumatics, Logic, Mathematics and Physics, by one Regent or Tutor, who also conducted them to church and examined them upon the sermons. This tutorial system was no doubt inadequate; but the amount of learning, especially in classical literature, which many of the students acquired shows that it had merits. After such a course, Ebenezer 'laureated in Arts,' and began a five-years' curriculum of theology, which gave little impulse or instruction.

Outside the University, however, there were events which set him a-thinking. In the year of his father's death, one of his fellow-students, Thomas Aikenhead, was hanged for heresy at the age of eighteen, with the full approval of the local Presbytery. He heard the General Assembly disputing in vain the King's title to alter its date of meeting, and submitting reluctantly to His Majesty's regulation of the terms on which Episcopalian ministers should be allowed to retain their parishes. Meanwhile he heard, from week to week, the protests of the leading Edinburgh ministers against the gradual subjection of the Assembly to the firm but mediating policy of Carstares, for the pulpit retained its freedom long after the Church courts were subdued. Like all keen divinity students of his day, he was an unflagging sermon-hearer, taking shorthand notes of every sermon and adding brief comments of his own. Those comments show that he was more concerned about theology than Church affairs, and that his sympathies with evangelical doctrine had already taken shape.

During the latter part of his college course he was

tutor and chaplain to the Earl of Rothes, who resided in Edinburgh in winter and on his estate in Fife in summer. Lord Rothes was an orthodox Presbyterian of the conservative school, and with him Ebenezer formed a lasting friendship, which proved of value to him afterwards. But the tutorship had more important results. At Rothes he made the acquaintance of Alison Turpie, the daughter of a solicitor in the neighbouring town of Leslie, and there too he came under the superintendence of the Presbytery of Kirkcaldy, by which he was 'licentiated' as a probationer on February 11, 1703. In the spring he preached three times in the vacant church of Portmoak, which was within five miles of Rothes, and on May 26 he was called to the vacancy by 'the heritors and elders, the parishioners acquiescing in the call.' He had great hesitation about accepting the charge, the church and the manse being in a neglected condition. The Presbytery, however, having measured his abilities and his character, was eager for his settlement, and offered him an Act of Transportability, which would entitle him to remove to another charge without any formal procedure. With this proviso, he accepted the call, and was ordained to the ministry and inducted to the parish on September 22, 1703, at the age of twenty-two. Five months later he was married to Alison Turpie, to whom he presently became debtor for guidance which, under God, gave his life its power.

Leaving him on the threshold of the ministry, we may follow the early course of his brother Ralph to the point when he too was ordained.

Ralph, who was eleven years of age when his father died, followed Ebenezer to Edinburgh University in 1699. The University had by this time revived; special improvements were introduced when, in 1703, Carstares became Principal; and Ralph, who was a studious boy, made good use of the improved education. His student letters, most of which are in Latin, are distinctly above the prevailing level of scholarship. His disposition was sentimental and meditative, and he had a turn for versification, which was reflected in the cadence of his prose style. Like Ebenezer, he was a zealous hearer of sermons, and he had the same admiration for preachers of the orthodox school, especially for the Rev. James Webster, the chief champion of strict doctrine, whose name will occur repeatedly in this volume. After 1703 he spent his vacations at Portmoak Manse, and there his religion was deepened in intercourse with his sister-in-law. That profound sense of sin, and of the saving providence of God, which was the staple of the Scottish religion of last century, took possession of him, and led him rapidly towards evangelical belief. This is his own meditation upon his school and college days :—

'I remembered the many instances of the Lord's favour to me, and my rebellions against Him. I began with His mercies to me in the womb and on the breast, in England, in my infancy; and in Scotland, at Rivelaw, and Chirnside, and Ayton, and Dunse, and Edinburgh, and Portmoak, and Culross, and Dunfermline. I took special notice of the Lord's drawing out my heart towards Him at my father's death, and yet how early my rebellions against Him began to work. I took special notice also of what took place upon my first going to Edinburgh to the College, in the burning of the Parliament Close ; and how mercifully the Lord preserved me, when He might have taken me away in my sin, amidst the flames of that burning, which, I can say, my own sins helped to kindle. I took notice of the kindness of God, in providing for me since my father's death, preserving my mother, and what He did in ordering good company for me in Edinburgh, and how He manifested Himself to be God unto me ; and also His kindness manifested at Portmoak, of which I was made to say, He pitied me yonder at the hillside, and yonder on the top of the mountain, and yonder in the valley, and yonder in the east room, and yonder in the west room, and yonder in the low room, when He made my heart to go after Him. And yet I acknowledged my fearful sinning against that Holy Spirit that was leading me, from time to time.'

This devout disposition was developed by a tutorship

which he held for five years in the household of a distant kinsman, Colonel John Erskine of Culross, son of Lord Cardross, a zealous Presbyterian and the leader of the orthodox party in the Assembly. His tutorial duties were discharged with a laborious piety.

'Being thoughtful about my concerns with respect to the family, and my duty therein, and towards the children committed to my trust, I went to seek counsel of the Lord how to carry, and was made, with intentness of spirit, while praying, to seek that the Lord might give me a sight of my sins, and was made with affection to beg this, because I sought nothing but what was for His glory, and sought it for the sake of Christ, and because without it I could not glorify Him either here or hereafter; with sweetness pleading also, because He had promised it in His gracious covenant, where He has promised the Spirit. And a little afterwards, I was made to beg that the Lord would assist and direct me in my carriage with respect to the family, and the children committed to my custody in some measure, praying that the Lord might take the glory of all to Himself, by helping me to my work, and profiting the children.'

One of the children for whom this prayer was proffered rose to become a great jurist, the author of the *Institutes of the Law of Scotland* and the father of Dr John Erskine, leader of the Evangelicals in the Established Church at the end of the eighteenth century.

Ralph remained at Culross as tutor for two years after he had finished his theological course, being kept back from the ministry by a deep sense of unworthiness; but Colonel Erskine and the parish minister, George Mair, to whom Boston also owed a heavy debt, urged him to proceed, and on June 8, 1709, he was 'licentiated' by the Dunfermline Presbytery. Still he adhered to his tutorship and refused to preach in vacancies till 1711, when he was called to the second charge of Dunfermline parish by the 'great plurality of heritors, magistrates, town council and elders.' He was ordained at Dunfermline on August 7, 1711, and soon after was married to Margaret Dewar, daughter of the Laird of Lassoddie.

Eight months after his ordination an Act of Queen Anne restored patronage. It is noteworthy that, like Ebenezer, he was ordained in the terms of the Revolution Settlement. Carstares was still the ruling spirit of the Assembly, although the death of William had lessened his influence at Court. Doctrinal divergences had not yet taken shape. The Act of Toleration had not been drafted. The idea of 'dissent' had barely been conceived. Neither of the brothers showed any sympathy with the protesting Cameronians. By conviction and temperament, as well as by descent and training, they were strongly attached to the Church of the Reformation as re-established in 1690, and they entered the ministry with the desire of building up that Church on its new foundation.

In character they differed greatly. The younger brother had gifts which would in any situation have brought him distinction. Versatile, sympathetic and genial, he possessed a naïve humour and a lively fancy which gave picturesqueness and interest to almost everything that he wrote. A keen critical faculty was tempered by warmth of affection and glowing devoutness, and, from the first, he showed that whole-hearted zeal for the truths of personal religion which rarely fails to lead to eminent service. Ebenezer, with fewer gifts of heart, had a more independent and a stronger mind. There was indeed a self-contained calmness about him which detached him to some extent from his acquaintances, and a habit of wider outlook had developed in the more varied experiences of his boyhood. In an ordinary period of history he might have spent his life as an honourable and useful parish minister, somewhat hindered in his usefulness by a cold stateliness; but the strain of events brought out the native force and decisiveness which qualify men to be leaders in times of confusion, and private religious influences determined the trend of his activity.

CHAPTER III

THE ERSKINES AS PARISH MINISTERS

PORTMOAK parish lies on the shore of Loch Leven, six miles from Kinross, and four miles from Leslie. It abounds in sites of antiquarian and religious interest. Within a few hundred yards of the old church the Fount of Scotland, a large well with crystal clear water, recalls the days when Roman soldiers slaked their thirst after battle. Close at hand are the ruins of a church and hospital, built by the Culdees on land presented to them by Macbeth. The island of St Serf, with its legends of St Kentigern and its records of Prior Andrew Wintoun, was within the bounds of the parish, and was indeed anciently called Insula Petmook. The castle on a larger island had for ten months been Queen Mary's prison, while John Knox had preached and dispensed the Sacrament in a cleft of the hills hard-by.

After the Reformation, part of the Portmoak Priory was used for the worship of the Reformed Church; but in 1659 a church and manse were built on the skirts of Bishop's Hill and close to Portmoak village, the largest of four little villages which are included in the parish. It was of these that Ebenezer Erskine took possession in 1703. The church no longer exists, having given place to a better building in 1832. The manse, which is now used as the minister's stable, was in the solid and cramped style of the period, but gave from almost all its windows lovely views of the eastward part of the parish, which is one of the most picturesque in lowland Scotland. During

Covenanting days Presbyterianism had been maintained in a stone and turf building at Scotland Well, and the earnest labours of two excellent ministers had, before Ebenezer's induction, brought all the parishioners back to Presbyterianism. The two principal heritors, Bruce of Annat and Douglas of Kirkness, gave the young minister a cordial welcome to their homes; and he settled down to his pastorate, anxious to fulfil his duties, but chiefly perplexed by the 'unhealthy stance' of the manse, which had no drainage and was too near the swampy margin of the loch.

According to his own account, he began his ministry without much zeal, 'callously and mechanically, being swallowed up in unbelief and in rebellion against God.' He 'looked upon the doctrine of Christ as stuff, and wearied of nothing so much as to read the history of Christ in the evangelists.' He 'thought the Gospels the most wearisome part of the Bible, because they always came over the same thing.' His sermons, which were long and formal, he repeated by rote, with his eyes fixed on a certain nail in the opposite wall. With allowance for some exaggeration in his recollections, it is clear that he was on the road to a spiritless ministry with no special outcome, when a complete change came over him through the influence of his wife. She was a nervous and emotional, but deeply religious girl, who in the first years of her married life found more response to her devout feelings in her student brother-in-law, Ralph, than in her calm and frigid husband. Legend ascribes the change to a conversation on 'the deep things of God' which Ebenezer overheard between these two from his study window; but the truth, as he himself narrates it, is more interesting than the legend. In 1807, after the birth of her second child, Mrs Erskine was seized with a fit of profound melancholia. Those were times when superstition marched close to religion. Ten years later the neighbouring manse of Kinross was occupied by evil spirits who carried away silver spoons, inserted pins into eggs, and resisted the prayers of the minister and his session for several months. But the spirit that haunted Portmoak was of another kind.

'The particular sin she complained of was her unbelief. The law of God, in its majesty, spirituality and authority, was set before her. For a month or two the arrows of the Almighty were within her, the poison whereof did drink up her spirits, and the terrors of God did set themselves in array against her. In those depths she continued, till the Lord moved me to call some neighbouring ministers to join in prayer on her behalf, particularly Mr Andrew Wardrope in the parish of Ballingry, Mr Andrew Thomson of Orwell, Mr John Shaw of Leslie and Mr John Currie of Kinglassie. Everyone of them prayed by turns with her in my closet and conversed with her ; but no relief appeared, until Mr Wardrope proposed that she should pray with them before they parted. She was exceedingly averse from it ; yet, being constrained to it, and being in an agony of spirit through the terrors of God, she at last complied.

' But oh ! that her words were now written and printed in a book, that they were graven with an iron pen and lead in the rock for ever ! For to the conviction of all present the Spirit of God spoke out of her. There was not, I suppose, a dry cheek among all the ministers or others of the family that were present. Her expressions were so full of the Spirit, so suited to the case of her soul, and in such heavenly eloquence, that if a General Assembly of ministers had compiled and studied it, it could not have been better digested. That same day the Lord was pleased to calm her spirit and break the strength of her temptation. He gave her a sweet serenity of mind, and helped her to a holy, tender and circumspect walk, and an humble waiting upon Him in the way of duty, both public and private, for many years. . . . This, I think, was the first time that ever I felt the Lord touching my heart in a sensible manner. Her distress and affliction, with her deliverance, were blessed to me. Some few weeks after, she and I were sitting together in my closet, and while we were conversing about the things of God, the Lord was pleased to rend the veil and to give me a glimmering view of salvation, which made my soul to acquiesce in Christ as the new and living way to glory.'

Though this was the beginning of his spiritual life, it was twelve months before he found a standing-ground.

A voluminous diary, which he began in 1707, shows that he passed through deep waters, tossed between the doctrines of grace and a very thorough scepticism. But in the summer of 1708 he 'got his head out of Time into Eternity,' and on August 26, a date which he cherished in grateful remembrance, God 'brought his heart to give a consent to Him,' and he became sure that God could never 'deny His own covenant.' The words of the original covenant have not been preserved, but we have it as it was renewed a few months later.

' Lord, if I have done iniquity, I am resolved through Thy grace to do so no more. I flee for shelter to the blood of Jesus and His everlasting righteousness; for this is pleasing unto Thee. I offer myself up, soul and body, unto God the Father, Son and Holy Ghost. I offer myself unto Christ the Lord, as an object proper for all His offices to be exercised upon. I choose Him as my Prophet, for instruction, illumination and direction. I embrace Him as my great Priest, to be washed and justified by His blood and righteousness. I embrace Him as my King, to reign and rule within me. I take a whole Christ, with all His laws, and all His crosses and afflictions. I except against none of them. I will live to Him; I will die to Him; I will quit with all I have in the world for His cause and truth. Only, Thou must be surety for me, and fulfil in me all the good pleasure of Thy goodness. Thou must fulfil both Thy own part and my part of this covenant; for this is the tenor of Thy covenant, "I will be their God, and they shall be my people; I will put my spirit within them, and cause them to walk in my statutes; when Thou passeth through the waters I will be with thee: I will never, never, never, leave thee nor forsake thee." Lord, upon these terms, I renew my covenant this night; and I take heaven and earth, angels and men, sun and moon and stars, the stones and timber of this house, to witness, that upon these terms, I give myself away, in soul and body and estate, and all I am or have in this world, unto God, Father, Son and Holy Ghost. And upon these terms I subscribe myself—Thy sworn servant for ever,

EB. ERSKINE.'

There was nothing proud or boastful in the faith which

he thus reached. Sometimes he was 'sadly in the dark, dead, hard and stupid, like a very stone.' His religion was clouded, or at least sobered, by recurring doubts, and as in the case of all strong minds his doubts were about the deepest and broadest truths. The Incarnation sometimes appeared to him as incredible. Sometimes he had 'fears that Jesus may have been an impostor.' For a long time he 'was tempted to doubt the immortality of the soul.' Such dubieties were recorded in his journal, and most of them were fully discussed with his wife. But faith steadily prevailed and gave him increasing clearness as to the 'freedom of the blessed way of salvation and the firmness of the blessed covenant.' He was in every sense a new man, and entered into a life of genuine but not austere devoutness. Rising habitually at 4 a.m. for prayer, he took guidance alternately from the Bible, open before him, and from the star-lit or cloudy sky stretched above Loch Leven. The 'glory of God in the heavens' was his favourite meditation, balanced by a quiet delight in the covenant he had made with the Creator, and his prayers always closed with intercession for his parishioners, for whose spiritual welfare he had now a new anxiety.

'This day I got my bonds in some measure loosed. Requests flowed in upon me, and I was helped to believe that the Lord would answer. I was made to pray for the members of Christ everywhere, particularly for Janet Paterson and Jean Raubit and my brother Ralph. . . . The Lord gave me some enlargement, to pray that I might be an instrument to build up a kingdom for Him among His people. . . . Having been abroad visiting my Lady Strenrie, I have been endeavouring to turn my thoughts towards soul-concerns. I have had some very awful impressions of eternity, which filled me with fear and consternation. However the fourth chapter of John's Gospel yielded me relief and enlargement. Oh wonderful ! the great God, who stretched out the heavens and laid the foundations of the earth, sitting in such a posture, *wearied* with a journey. I was made to pray that I may have furniture from Him for the edification of His mystical body. I bear His commission, and therefore I believe He will be with me.'

'I had this day, in going about in the ground of Annat, a solid impression of God upon my spirit and of the great worth of precious souls. That I may speak suitable words to them, Lord, grant me the tongue of the learned to commend Thee, with a suitable ballast of humbling and sanctifying grace.'

The following extracts from his journal show the rigour and realism of his self-scrutiny :—

'Aug. 20, 1714.—This evening, while I was shearing some tobacco to be snuff, I had a check for my excesses in the use of it, and that because, in my last fever, I resolved to leave it, and because what I spend in this way, if bestowed in charity, would do good to some of the poor people of God ; and, besides, I am too much under the power of it. I again resolved that I will be more moderate in the use of it, and, if I can, I will endeavour to quit it altogether. . . . Oh, Lord, kill every lust and idol in my heart by the virtue of the blood of the Lamb.'

'Nov. 8, 1714.—Through grace I am resolved to fulfil my vow to the Lord and to quit the use of snuff, except I see some evil consequence and fruit, prejudicial to my health or sight or the like : for I reckon that, in that case, it would be sin to me *not* to use it, as a medicine. Man was never designed to serve any creature, which we become guilty of, when we are so wedded to the use of it that we cannot want it, though the necessity of nature does not call for it. It is an inverting of the very order of nature, when man becomes a slave to any inferior creature : for God did put all things under his feet, to be as it were his servants. . . . I find it necessary for me that I keep my soul in its room and my body in its own room also. I must use this creature, only in a subservient way.'

One would hope that the 'creature,' in however subservient a way, was allowed without injuring conscience to serve him as a medicine, for at this very date he entered a period of trouble in which both body and soul were in need of healing. He was laid low with fever, and after hanging for a year on the verge of the grave, recovered only to face a series of losses which shook and strained his whole character. Three young children and a dearly loved sister died within two months; his wife's health gave way; and of the remaining children— his family had increased to ten—one after another was seized with fever or small-pox. The heritors with all their friendliness would not see to the drainage of the manse, and at last, in 1720, he was left a widower, his wife being rapidly followed to the grave by Isabel, the favourite daughter of the household. He had strong family affections, and his diary tells tale after tale of struggle.

'My pleasant child, Ebenezer, is at this moment laying in fever, and I have been entreating the Lord for him. The answer I have got is a discovery of God and His sovereignty which fills me with dread, and stops my mouth, that I dare not quarrel whatever be the issue. My soul adheres and cleaves to Him, like the weak ivy to the strong oak. . . . While my heart was clasping and gripping the child, the Lord bade me loose my grips and suffer Eben to come to Him. Whereupon my soul sweetly echoed back again, "Lord, if Thou hast use for him in Thy heavenly kingdom, I quit him with more than a thousand good-wills, for he is Thine own, and why should'st Thou not have Thine own? Thou hast given Thine only Son, out of love to the like of me, and shall not I cheerfully give my son to Thee when Thou callest for him?"'

'I had a particular affection for Isabel, and doted but too much upon her, because she was the likest her mother of any of the children, both as to her countenance and humour. But I see that the Lord will not allow me to have any idols, but will have the whole of my heart to Himself. . . .

'I remember that, a day or two before the child fell sick, she was in my closet. She and I being alone, I took her on my knee and dandled her, and she was very fond of me, took me round the neck and kissed me; which engaged my heart very much. But my love and affection to the child filled me with a strong desire to have Christ formed in her soul, and thereupon I began to commend Christ to her. The Lord helped me to speak in such words as were suitable to her capacity, to which she seemed very attentive. Particularly I told her, I remember, that she would die, and that it would be better to die and to go to heaven where Christ is, and where she would meet with her dear mother, than to be here; at which words the dear child gave a broad look in my face, as if she had been taken with the thing. I bless the Lord who put it in my heart and mouth to converse with her at that time.'

'I take it kindly that the Lord comes to my family to gather lilies, wherewith to garnish the upper sanctuary, for of such is the Kingdom of Heaven. And oh! it sometimes affords me a pleasing prospect, to think that I have so much plenishin in heaven before me, and that, when I enter the gates of glory, I shall not only be welcomed by the whole general assembly of saints and angels, but my wife and four pleasant babes will, in a particular manner, welcome me to those regions.'

Those sorrows coincided with heavy public responsibilities, but he was unflagging in his ministry, and developed it in several new directions. He increased and organised the work of his elders, binding them to official fidelity and to personal devoutness by a series of testing questions, to which they submitted every six months. It is noteworthy, in view of later events, that he initiated the practice of having the elders elected by the vote of the parishioners. He also originated Praying Societies in different districts of the parish, and drew up rules for giving their meetings a definite value and a distinct connection with the Church. He brought the parish school into a state of high efficiency, being assisted by an able teacher, under whom the school produced at least two pupils of note, John Mair the Latinist, and Michael Bruce the poet. On Sundays all the children of the parish met in the Schoolhouse, to be examined by him on the day's sermons and the Catechism, forming perhaps the first Sunday School on record. His public spirit was conspicuous, especially when the religion of the nation was in question. In 1707 he roused the antagonism of extremists by giving thanks in church for the Union of the Kingdoms, and in 1715 he organised his parishioners as a volunteer corps. His spiritual awakening led him into a crusade against the license of Penny Weddings and other rustic immoralities. Nor did he spare the rich. In one page of his diary there is a prayer for courage to rebuke the Laird of —— for frequenting the tavern during the hours of public worship, and the prayer was not in vain. Yet graciousness tempered his strictness. 'Peace be unto this house' was his habitual greeting when he entered the humblest cottage, and the little children had no terror of his strict catechising. Gradually his hold of the people was strengthened, until, after twenty years' ministry, he could report to the Presbytery that in the whole parish there was not one dissenter.

The pulpit, however, was the centre, and the gospel was the spring, of his influence. Immediately after his conversion his method of preaching changed. Stiff and dogmatic formality gave place to calmness and freedom. His hearers noted that his eyes were no longer fixed on a single spot, but moved from face to face with affectionate earnestness. In his style there was no rhetorical exuberance, such as Hill Burton ascribes to him. It was limpid, consecutive and forcible, comparatively free from illustration, and redundant only through incessant quotation of Scripture. The mark of his manner was dignity. With massive, regular features, bearing the stamp of his birth, and a vigorous well-set frame, he conveyed an idea of power by his very appearance, and in his delivery, even when most excited, he maintained a stately but simple graciousness. One of his bitterest ecclesiastical opponents is reported to have said, 'You never heard Ebenezer Erskine! Well, sir, you never heard the gospel in its majesty.' But the strength of his preaching lay in its substance. Without expressly discarding the doctrine of election, he called his hearers to set it aside, as a 'matter with which they had no more concern than with what men are doing in Mexico and Peru,' and gave out the

Good News with that clearness and fulness to which the predestinarianism of Scotland has never prevented a response. Of all the sermons which have been preserved by his 'scribes,' as he affectionately styled the short-hand writers who clustered round the pulpit, not one fails to repeat the free offer of grace to all without distinction. Although modern ears are accustomed to this, it was exceedingly rare in those times. Rarer still it was that the 'offer' should rest on a basis of solid reasoning.

As early as 1714 the parish church proved too small for the crowds that gathered on Sundays, and even at a Thursday evening Lecture, which he instituted, it was always full. Except in wild weather, he preached in an adjacent field. 'To-day,' he writes, 'the church would not hold the half; the people heard with a great deal of greediness and attention, so as if they would have drawn the word out of me.' At Communions more than 2000 persons, drawn from all parts of Fife, were usually present, and when he assisted in other parishes the attendance was as large. Preaching was the delight of his life, and when, in course of years, the doctrines he preached were condemned by Church Courts, the sense of his being under ban gave him a new zeal and his hearers a new zest.

'It is my desire in every place to send forth the savour of that Name which is as ointment poured forth; and I look on it as my crown, my glory and my joy, when He helps me in any measure to commend Him unto souls. Oh, pray for me, that I may be honoured and helped to make His praise glorious; for it is the greatest credit ever a poor creature came to, to be a trumpet to send forth the joyful sound of life, liberty, and salvation through Him.'

'After reading Mr Rutherford's Dying Testimony to the work of God in the land, and two or three of his letters, I got liberty, when laying over the window with my little daughter Jeanie, and when looking up to the heavens, to commend the glorious Creator, and in particular the Bright and Morning Star, and to speak in His name. It is the desire of my soul to make His name to be remembered in all generations.'

In the neighbouring parishes the ministers as a rule were of the orthodox school, and with all of them, except for a brief period afterwards to be named, he was for twenty years on intimate and friendly terms. The Presbytery and, so far, the county became noted as a religious centre, attractive to young men of evangelical views and obnoxious to the leaders of the parliamentary party. Erskine was the outstanding figure in the district. Till 1725 he published no sermons, but his Sacramental preaching steadily extended his reputation. He often preached in Edinburgh, especially in the pulpit of Mr Webster of the Tolbooth Parish, whose daughter he married in 1724 as his second wife, and his doctrinal views brought him into prominence in the General Assembly. He was repeatedly called to larger parishes. Some of the calls were blocked by heritors and by presbyteries on account of his doctrines; others he himself set aside. It was not till 1731, when he had been twenty-seven years at Portmoak, that he saw reasons for making a change. In that year he accepted a call to the Third Charge of Stirling, which had previously been held by James Guthrie, the first of those who suffered martyrdom after the Restoration. Gossips ascribed the change to the dislike of his town-bred wife to the seclusion of a rustic manse; but it is more likely that he felt he was called to take a central position in view of the impending crisis. In bidding farewell to his parishioners, amidst demonstrations of their affectionate sorrow, he chose as his text: 'I go bound in the spirit to Jerusalem, not knowing the things that shall befall me there.' It is equally significant that, when he approached the Royal Burgh, the Provost and Magistrates came out to meet him in procession. Since the days of Guthrie, Stirling had had evangelical ministers,

THE ERSKINES 41

and he was welcomed, not only as one of the most impressive preachers of a 'free gospel,' but as a man who had courage, skill and power to defend his beliefs.

Meanwhile the ministry of Ralph had also developed. Dunfermline at the time of his ordination had 5000 'communicable persons,' and was already famed for its linen industry; but religiously it was all but dead. There was only one church, and from 1705 till 1710 there had been no minister, the Episcopalian incumbent having been deposed for Arianism and neglect of duty. For many years the Sacraments had not been observed, and the Kirk-session was extinct. Ralph cordially joined the minister of the First Charge, who had been ordained nine months before him, in the upbuilding of the church according to the manner of the time. Deacons and elders were at once ordained, and initiated in their duties, among which was included the perambulation of the town during church hours with a posse of policemen, in order to compel attendance. Every household in the parish was visited and examined annually. Fellowship meetings were instituted in different districts. Collections for the poor were appointed. Subscriptions were gathered for missions to the Highlands and to America. Classes for the young were formed, and a Catechism was drawn up for their use—the first cheerful question being, 'Are you so young that you may not be sick and die?' and the second, 'Are you so young that you may not go to hell?' Within two years the church was crowded, and the Communions were attended by 4000 or 5000 church members. This revival was local, but it was genuine and permanent, and the instrument of it was Ralph's preaching.

As a preacher, he had remarkable gifts. With a lively and piquant fancy he combined a scholar's habits, which prevented exuberance and repetition. A real master in the steady and skilful use of illustration, he moved rapidly from point to point in pursuit of his purpose—the clear presentation of central Christian truths. He was emphatically a man with a well-ordered creed, and he continually referred to the Confession and Catechisms. Yet his ordinary preaching was not argumentative. Some of the allegorical and devotional passages in his sermons recall Rutherford; but he had a practical sense and an edge of humour, which saved him from Rutherford's excesses. From egoism he was absolutely free, and he showed a settled dislike for self-analysis. His doctrines were broadened and enlarged by his national feeling. The creed which he commended was an historical one, and he was filled with a desire to defend and deepen the religion of Scotland. His expositions were the outcome of good Greek and Hebrew scholarship, which he had reached by unremitting study, and of a general culture rare in those days. Yet to his hearers the chief novelty and charm of his sermons lay in their homely and personal appeals. Like his brother, he habitually told them that Election was a 'secret thing that belonged to God,' and that their one business was to close with Christ. He had drunk at the fountain of free grace at an earlier age than Ebenezer, and in his preaching he had more liberty and glow. Critics have sometimes quoted with reprobation his descriptions of eternal punishment, but these differed from the language of his contemporaries only in their exhibition of a more vivid imagination. There was a far greater distinction in his unfailing appendix, that the tortures described might be avoided by all his hearers. When he turned from invitation to meditation, the idea of a hell reserved for all but believers vanished. Only a superficial reader will say that the damnation of unbaptised children was part of the creed of the man, who wrote :—

> In heavenly choirs a question rose
> That stirred up strife will never close,
> What rank of all the ransomed race
> Owes highest praise to sovereign grace?

> Babes, thither caught from womb and breast,
> Claimed right to sing above the rest,
> Because they found the happy shore
> They never saw nor sought before.

No one who turns from the prosy and laboured platitudes of the Moderates, or the heavy reasonings of the traditional predestinarians, to 'Pregnant Promise and her Issue, being Seven Sermons by Ralph Erskine, mostly preached on Sacramental Occasions,' will wonder that there was a revival of religion at Dunfermline, or that such volumes were eagerly read throughout Scotland, and were welcomed in England as a foretaste of the message not yet delivered by the Wesleys. Two or three brief extracts will give some idea of his method :

'There are some birds, when there is a moorburn,[1] they will flutter over their young when they are in hazard of being burnt, even till they burn themselves. O, sirs, sin raised a great moorburn, a great fire, the fire of hell, the fire of God's wrath. All the children of promise, as well as the rest of the world, were like to be burnt in that moorburn. Christ came down, flying on the wings of love, in our flesh, and fluttered over His young, till He was burnt to death in the fire : but being God as well as man, He rose again, and brought all His children out of the fire with Him : and now, all that are actually children of promise have such an impress of His love stamped on them, that they have some conformity to Him in His love.'

'Some are taken up warring against this or that lust, but in vain while they never strike at the sinful nature that is in them. You may beat down the bitter fruit of an ill tree till you be weary ; but while the root is never touched, it will bring forth more ; if the tree be not made good, the fruit will never be good ; it is the good Spirit of God that makes a good tree. Do not think that, when you bear down a particular lust for a while about (at the time of) a sacrament, you are a mortified man. Nay, it is but like the making of a dam against the water ; it may silence the noise of the stream, for a while that the dam is agathering, but it increases upon your hand, and will come down afterwards with the more violence. So here, there will be but

---

[1] *i.e.* When the heather is on fire.

little success in subduing particular sins, and mortifying certain individual lusts, while the fountain of all corruption remains unstruck at and unmortified. True mortification and warring against sin differ as much from that as the sun painted on a wall differs from the sun in the firmament.'

'As you know, one great pipe or conduit for water to a city may have many branches and lesser pipes, for conducting the water to this or that part of the city, and even to private houses, for the benefit of particular persons, according as the contrivance is ordered. Behold, here is a contrivance of infinite wisdom, from the great conduit of the covenant that stands fast in Christ Jesus. There are many pipes-full of water for refreshing, full of wine for cheering, full of milk for nourishing souls. And we are come to set the pipe to your mouth : "Ho, everyone that thirsteth, come to the waters." Here is a pipe for every mouth, by which you may draw in Christ to your heart, though He be in heaven, and you on earth.'

'What ! will you prefer a black devil, a base world, a brutish lust, before Christ and all His promises of grace and glory ? O God forbid ! Fy for shame ! will you reject the word of grace, the promise of mercy that God is putting into your mouth by this glorious gospel ? O better chuse to die upon the spot, than lose such a sweet morsel, a taste of grace, and a foretaste of glory. You shall not have it to say that you came to Glendovan such a day, and got nothing ; for I take you all witnesses, and heaven and earth to witness, that you have got an offer of grace, of Christ, and a promise that is worth ten thousand worlds.'

He had a rare gift of speaking tenderly and helpfully to people at the Communion Table. Here are a few sentences from one of his appeals :—

'Perhaps there is some trembling, weak believer here, that is doubting whether he has grace or not, and fearing he has no interest in the Man that is God's Fellow. Tell me, will you quit your part of Him ? Could you freely choose to take the world and your lusts, and let others take Christ who please ? Would you find in your heart to rest contented with other things, and give to anybody your part in Christ ? What say you to that, poor, doubting soul ? Is your heart now melting and relenting within you, and saying, "O minister, what is that you are asking, that wounds me to the bottom of my soul? Quit all my part in Christ! Oh, no, no, no! I would not quit my part in Him for ten thousand, thousand worlds; and even as it is, though I dare not say I have an interest in Him, yet I would not say that I would quit my part in Him; no, not for all that lies within the bosom of the universe." Is that the language of your heart? Well, Christ hears that, and He will mind it as a token of some heart-kindness to Him.'

On the death of his colleague in 1715, he was promoted by the Presbytery to the First Charge of the parish, 'at the request of the heritors, magistrates, town-councillors and elders, none of the parishioners objecting.' In the filling of the vacancy caused by his promotion, a contest arose, which occupied his attention for three years and prepared him for future struggles. It well illustrates the condition of Church affairs. The patron of the parish, with the approval of the heritors, appointed a Mr Christie. Patronage was now the law of the land; but the Presbytery declared that it was contrary to the principles of the Church of Scotland, and proceeded to consult the heritors, magistrates and parishioners. They objected to the settlement of Christie, and the Presbytery declined to induct him; whereupon he appealed to the Assembly. After two years of altercation between Assembly and Presbytery, a compromise was secured, by the Assembly's Commission submitting four names to the parishioners, for their choice. But, when the parishioners met, they elected a man outside the leet submitted, a Mr James Wardlaw, and the Presbytery proceeded to ordain Wardlaw as Ralph's colleague. So the Presbytery and the people had their way, and the Supreme Court proved its unwillingness or its inability to support the patron.

Like most of the popular candidates in disputed settlements, Wardlaw was an evangelical, and Ralph gave him an ardent welcome to Dunfermline. The colleagues signed an amusingly minute covenant—all things in those days were covenanted—in order to prevent strife. Among other agreements, they undertook that neither would 'yield to the management of his wife,' and that 'if any commended the one beyond the other, he would drop what might create discouragement to his colleague as occasion allowed.' The covenant was thoroughly successful in its purpose. Wardlaw loyally supported the work of his gifted colleague. Neither wives nor flatterers created difficulty between them, and their cordiality was undisturbed till ecclesiastical variance arose.

Personally, indeed, Ralph was a man with whom it would have been hard to quarrel. Geniality and affectionateness marked all his social relations. He was a wit, a raconteur, the possessor of many friends in every rank of life. He played the violin with skill, and stories were repeated of the comical sadness with which his grave elders admitted that he was 'nane the waur for his tunes on the wee sinful fiddle.' In 1719 he wrote to his Episcopalian half-brother Philip, proposing a 'fraternal correspondence' and expressing his belief—a rare one in those days—that between the two Churches of which they were ministers there was no essential difference 'as regards eternal salvation,' so long as Episcopalians adhered to the Thirty-nine Articles. 'He shall not strive nor cry' was one of his favourite quotations, and one of his guiding rules. When drawn into public controversy, he showed more keenness and acerbity than his brother, but this was due to his warmer disposition. Indeed his nieces wrote to him with more freedom than to their own father, and, in the sorrows which fell upon the Portmoak manse, he always appeared as a cheery counsellor. One of those consolatory visits was the occasion of a poem which had great vogue at the time. He had joined a number of neighbours who, according to custom, kept night-watch over the remains of one of his nieces. 'The conversation,' writes a parishioner who was present, 'was exceedingly instructive and refreshing. In an interval Mr Ralph gave us 'Smoking Spiritualised.' The verses were not quite original, being based upon a seventeenth century poem, but they have a quaintness of their own, especially as having been extemporised in such circumstances.

Was this small plant for thee cut down?
So was the Plant of great renown,
Which mercy sends
For nobler ends:
Thus think, and smoke tobacco.

Doth juice medicinal proceed
From such a naughty, foreign weed?
Then what's the power
Of Jesse's flower?
Thus think, and smoke tobacco.

The promise, like the pipe, inlays,
And by the mouth of faith conveys
What virtue flows
From Sharon's Rose:
Thus think, and smoke tobacco.

In vain the unlighted pipe you blow;
Your pains in outward means are so,
Till heavenly fire
Your heart inspire:
Thus think, and smoke tobacco.

The smoke, like burning incense, towers;
So should a praying heart of yours
With ardent cries
Surmount the skies:
Thus think, and smoke tobacco.

His sister-in-law's death in 1720 prompted an effusion of the same type, which is engraved on her tombstone:—

The Law brought forth its precepts ten,
And then dissolved in grace ;
This saint ten children bore, and then
In glory took her place.

His own family life overflowed with affection. He was twice married [1] and had fourteen children. To them he was passionately attached and their spiritual welfare was constantly in his thoughts.

' 1733 (?) In the evening I was helped to pray particularly in behalf of Peggy, whom I was designing to send to Edinburgh. My heart was poured out before God, in view of His covenant, that He would be with her and keep her.

' June 27, 1734. This evening Peggy spoke with me, desiring my prayers weeping, and saying she could pray none. Some time ago I had bid her think of the Sacrament. I was glad to get the commission from her, and when I was alone I got grace to pray particularly, with my soul melting before God.'

' July 19, 1735. I preached this day at the Kinglassie Sacrament and served eight Tables. While I served the fifth or sixth, I saw my daughter Peggy at the Table before me ; and then the word "thy God and the God of thy seed" coming in mind, my heart was led to look to God in her behalf ; and being much helped and strengthened in serving that Table, I was thereafter somewhat quickened.'

' June 24, 1734.—This morning, after looking to the Lord in prayer, and going with the family to ordinances (at Carnock), I heard for a while Mr Wardrope's sermon on that text, "The cup which My Father hath given Me, shall I not drink it?" In the midst of the sermon an express, sent by my wife, came from Dunfermline, telling me of Ralphie's being threatened with death. I called my servant to get the horse, and sat hearing till the sermon was done, which I thought was very suitable to me, and which I heard with some application. He gave out Ps. xxiii. at the close, which I was helped to sing with some pleasure and melting of soul. When I came home, the child was no worse.'

' Sept. 18.—My child Ralph was still weaker. I joined with my

---

[1] His second wife was Margaret Simson, daughter of a Writer to the Signet.

colleague, this day, in prayer for him, and for fruit by this rod to me and my wife, whom I found somewhat exercised, and brought to some submission to the Lord's will. About the middle of the day, I got him again cast over on the covenant. . . . I was led to acknowledge the Lord was righteously angry with me, and to seek He might pity me, that I might never grieve His Spirit again. After this, I prayed beside the child and the company, and was therein helped to some exercise of the same kind as in secret, and a little while after, about eight o'clock, *my child Ralph died.* I endeavoured meantime to comfort my wife; and after his death, going to my closet, I got some grace to acknowledge the holiness, righteousness, mercy and faithfulness of God, and had some confidence exercised in Him as a promising God, notwithstanding His slaying dispensation. My heart was especially poured out, and mightily melted, in praying for the blessing of this rod to my wife and me, that it might be truly sanctified, and made a mean of the Lord's accomplishing His word of grace, on which He had caused me to hope; that it might be a mean of purging away my dross; and that it might be blessed to the family, particularly to the servant Jean, who had waited carefully on the child.'

The direct and loving religion of his household life had its counterpart in his relations with his elders, whom he bound together in habits of united prayer and fasting. To his parishioners he was a confiding and trusted friend, and, beyond the parish, the circle of persons to whom he acted as spiritual adviser gradually widened. In this capacity he made a literary departure, which greatly increased his reputation and his influence. From early boyhood he had, for his own relaxation, indulged in the habit of verse-making; and when doctrinal controversies arose, he resolved to utilise his gift by issuing a rhythmical statement of evangelical truth. In 1726 he published a slim volume of ' Gospel Canticles,' which was enlarged and re-published a few years later as ' Gospel Sonnets,' with amendments suggested by Isaac Watts, who was one of his correspondents. In the prefaces, which varied from edition to edition, he disclaimed the idea of being an original poet, and stated that his aim was the religious

D

edification of his congregation, his friends, and any others whom the sonnets might reach.

'The songs are spiritual, set out in the midst of a carnal and corrupt age, most part whereof will indeed never bestow a glance of their eye upon them, and therefore their censure needs not be feared ; or, if they do, it is like it may be with contempt of them, in comparison of wanton and profane sonnets.'

His expectation as to the literary verdict was to some extent fulfilled. The songs were rapidly written, and contained frequent irregularities, both in rhyme and in metre. They abounded in quips, antitheses and para-doxes, and they were burdened with proof-texts. In some editions every line had its Scriptural proof, showing that the author was far more concerned for doctrinal cor-rectness than for literary effect. It would be easy to quote ludicrous couplets, and it would be difficult to quote many which have permanent merit. Yet as a whole they were forcible and impressive ; and to a generation in which poetry was a rare and never very splendid plant, and which was accustomed to a tedious and formal presentation of religious truth, they seemed fresh, and even beautiful. Ralph himself would probably have smiled if he had been called a poet, but he might have smiled in another way if anyone had hinted that he had failed in his scheme. The sonnets carried their message to those who had no mind for argument, and they travelled far further than he or his friends anticipated. When George Whitefield was in America he wrote : 'Your sonnets have been blessed to me, and to many here.'

It is impossible, within the limits of this volume, to give an adequate account of Ralph's unique and almost romantic ministry. It was quaint without eccentricity, and picturesque without irregularity. Pervaded by deep piety, it had not a shade of gloom. There was far more variety in it than in that of Ebenezer, and until the tide of events brought them into troubled waters, Ralph exercised a larger influence, and had a wider reputation. Yet he was not made of so firm a fibre. His playful and meditative disposition disinclined him to act promptly except under strong pressure of conscience, while his sensitive spirit of reverence made him very conservative. But for his brother's initiative, he would have died parish minister of Dunfermline. In the following pages he will appear in a secondary place. Yet the hope may be hazarded that, with the revival of interest in eighteenth century Scotland, some competent student will not grudge the pains needed to present a full-length portrait of one of the few men of that period who had real individuality, bordering upon genius.

CHAPTER IV

THE RISING STORM

THE Erskines were not only devoted ministers of the Church of Scotland. They accepted and advocated, in their early ministry, the prevailing ideas of National Religion. While not regarding the Revolution Settlement as more than a phase or an epoch in the continuous life of the Reformed Church, they held that it supplied conditions under which the nation might foster and defend the Church, in her purity and freedom. They attached grave consequence to the recognition of the 'true religion' by the State, and were in consequence intensely loyal to the Hanoverian dynasty. From this attitude they never swerved. But the logic of events altered their perspective. Unwillingly, if not unwittingly, they were led to regard the purity and freedom of the Church as imperilled by existing relations. The course of Church affairs came home to them at four points, viz. : (1) The direct and indirect interference of the State with the rights of the Church; (2) the working of Patronage, when accepted and enforced by the General Assembly; (3) the unchecked growth of erroneous doctrine, within the Church; (4) the suppression of individual liberty to contend and protest against those evils.

In 1711 Parliament began to meddle in several ways with the Revolution Settlement and with the understanding on which the Union of 1707 had been effected; but it was from the Toleration Act of January 11, 1712, that disturbance first arose in Scotland. More offensive

52

than the Act itself was the Oath of Abjuration which it imposed upon all ministers, Presbyterian as well as Episcopalian. The Oath referred explicitly to an Act in favour of the 'Princess Sophia and the heirs of her body,' in which the Crown was secured, not to Protestants as Protestants—in that limitation Scotland would have cordially concurred—but to communicants of the Church of England. When ministers were enjoined, under civil penalties, to take the Oath on or before November 1, the indignation in Scotland was widespread and found voice in the Assembly; but the Assembly's protest was spiritless and ineffectual, and as a rule parish ministers took the Oath reluctantly. In almost every Presbytery there were stalwarts, who resolutely declined. The Erskines were of this number. In April Ebenezer wrote : 'The power and policy of hell is set to work for the ruin and overthrow of the Church of Scotland. . . . I should be glad to know what our ministers are thinking about this Oath, though I am resolved not to make any man my standard, even if I be driven to beg bread.' Six months later he was 'distressed to find that two-thirds of the ministers had agreed to take the Oath.' His own determination was firm. On October 30 he and his neighbour, Currie of Kinglassie, obtained leave of absence from the Presbytery, in order to avoid the threatened penalty. The danger passed ; Government shrank at the last moment from enforcement of the Act, and Erskine returned to his work. But a divergence, which afterwards widened, had arisen within the Presbytery. Once and again he used language in the pulpit, which his neighbours resented, about 'men who juggled with God in solemn oaths, and would not run the risk of displeasing kings and queens and potentates and parliaments.' When the Oath was reimposed in a modified form, in 1715, he at first agreed to take it. 'His foot,' he writes, 'had well-nigh slipped, but mercy held him up'; and he again declined. The loyalty shown by parish ministers in the '15 led to a further modification of the Oath, and there was no definite attempt to enforce compliance, the matter being left with the Presbyteries, which acted variously in accordance with the spirit which prevailed in each locality.

Ralph, also, refused to take the Oath. To him it would have meant the abandonment of a visionary hope, which Ebenezer's shrewder mind had never cherished, that Britain might one day become Presbyterian. Yet his chief objection was to the Erastianism of the action of the Government. How little violence entered into his view of the subject is shown in some verses which he addressed to the King, and of which the following is a fair specimen :—

> 'Though all could freely, without laws to urge,
> Abjure the popish James, and swear to George;
> Yet while it swelled with circumstantial clauses,
> Old English Acts reduplicating *as*'s,
> Some feared to leave their conscience in the lurch
> And make the *kirk* to swear unto the *church*.
> Great nursing-father of our church and nation,
> Give an abortive birth to this temptation;
> 'Tis such a fertile womb of altercation.
> Our church, upon the whole, does well agree;
> But Oaths add little to its harmony.'

Concurrently with those controversies, which in themselves would have led to nothing, graver anxieties were rising, as the result of the restoration of patronage. In April 1712 Ebenezer wrote : 'I hear that the Bill for restoring patronages is passed the House of Commons. What a bold stroke is thus given to the fundamental constitution of the Church of Scotland!' In 1715 he was one of twenty-eight ministers who tendered a special protest against patronage, as 'subversive of the right of election belonging to Christian congregations by the

Word of God.' The Assembly, however, and the Presbyteries, were for a while unanimous in opposing the new law, and in seeking to cancel its provisions. Ebenezer carried his Presbytery with him in a declaration that, 'since the relation of pastor to people is plainly founded on the election, choice, or free consent of the people, they would go into no settlement, but where the people had freedom in electing their ministers.' Once, in 1717, the Presbytery departed from this pledge in deference to strong local influences, and he and Currie, when they lodged a protest, were publicly insulted by the angry patron. To this Erskine responded in a sermon. 'Heavy yokes are being wreathed about the Church's neck. . . . Christ's prerogative is invaded. . . . The Church owns no other head but Christ.' Yet the contention went no further, and in 1719 the efforts of the Assembly secured a modification of the Bill, which robbed it of its sting. Presentations were declared to be void, unless they were accepted by the presentees, and, in face of the strong and almost universal feeling of presbyteries and congregations, ministers and probationers did not venture to accept presentations in which congregations had not concurred. Students of church records say that from 1719 till 1729 there was not a single instance of a settlement without a call. At this stage, it will be observed, the Erskines were on the side which was not only popular but for a time victorious. Each in his Presbytery—Ebenezer at Kirkcaldy, and Ralph at Dunfermline in the more specific contest narrated in the last chapter—successfully advocated the rights of congregations, and the General Assembly, although hesitating and timid, acquiesced. As long as this was the case, the idea of separation from the Church did not enter their minds. It never occurred to them to be offended with the Church because of laws passed in London. Their one anxiety was that the Church should be loyal to her principles.

It was with regard to doctrine that divergences first assumed a permanent shape. The Arianism, which was rife in England at the beginning of the eighteenth century, had no real equivalent in Scotland. Of theology in the strict sense there was none. Scholarly research or progressive thinking can scarcely be said to have existed. Yet there was a tendency to move away from the rigours of the previous century without direct antagonism to the Confession of Faith. The new frankness with which Boston of Ettrick, Hog of Carnock and the Erskines preached the doctrines of grace was faced by an unwillingness to accept those doctrines in their completeness, which earned the name of Neonomianism. A strange school this latter was—predestinarian and forensic in its theory, yet prone to vague moralising, and disposed to tolerate anything but evangelical earnestness. Every man was 'saved' or 'lost'; but salvation was secondary to decent behaviour, and no man had any right to meddle with another man's opinions. It was enough to be willing to 'accept the Confession of Faith.' Underneath this equivocation, as Dr John Ker has said, there ran a definite tendency to exalt the ethical side of the Bible at the expense of the evangelical, and to deprive morality itself of its Christian meaning and motives. Those ideas produced no writer of mark, but they dominated the Assembly, and determined its policy for nearly half a century. They were first expressed in 1714, when Simson, a Glasgow professor of divinity, was charged with Arminianism by the Rev. James Webster of the Tolbooth, Ebenezer Erskine's father-in-law. Simson had a shifting and pretentious mind, and a distinct lack of courage. When brought to book, he avowed belief in the traditional theology, and disclaimed every special heresy alleged against him. The Assembly was satisfied with affirming that he 'had vented opinions not necessary to be taught in divinity, and had used misunderstood expressions, and with prohibiting him from using such expressions, and from venting such opinions.' The natural dissatisfaction of the evangelicals with this verdict was increased when, in 1717, the Assembly censured the Presbytery of Auchterarder for declaring that it was 'not sound or orthodox to teach that a man must forsake sin before coming to Christ.' In response to this censure which seemed to ignore the truth that Christ died for sinners, Hog of Carnock, on behalf of his party, brought out a Scottish edition of the *Marrow of Modern Divinity*, a book of which nine editions had appeared in England, since its publication in 1646, without giving rise to any controversy.[1] The Marrow, as it was popularly styled, was a clear and concise, though not an original exposition of the doctrine of Justification by Faith. The aim of its author, Edward Fisher, an Oxford graduate and the son of an English knight, was to clear away all the barriers which conscience and creeds raise between God's redeeming mercy in Christ and the soul of man. Its method of statement was antithetic, and some of the antitheses had a dubious sound, while there were doctrinal exaggerations in it of the kind which critics of evangelism always resent. It is not surprising that when, in 1720, it was brought under the notice of the Assembly, the prevalence of Neonomianism led to its being condemned, for the essence of its teaching was that a sinner could instantaneously be saved through acceptance of the gospel. Nor is it strange that the Erskines, to whom that doctrine was dear, took a place among twelve ministers, headed by Boston, who protested against the decision of the Assembly. Those twelve expressed their views in a Representation, drafted by Boston and revised by Ebenezer Erskine, in which, without

---

[1] It had been incidentally discovered by Boston in visiting one of his parishioners. Finding that it gave him 'light in darkness,' he transmitted it to Hog.

endorsing all the teaching of the *Marrow*, they begged
the Assembly to recall a decision which discredited some
leading truths of Christianity. The Assembly, however,
turned upon the 'Marrowmen,' and subjected them to
cross-examination on their own creed, proposing twelve
crucial questions to them. It fell to Ebenezer to prepare
the answers, and in discharging the task he gave the
first formal proof of the strength and lucidity of his
intellect. The Answers, which secured a place in the
history of Scottish theology, gave a clear, cogent and
catholic presentation of the Gospel, couched in worthy
language. Yet the Assembly was unmoved, and the
Representers or Marrowmen were, in 1722, rebuked
and admonished at the bar. Thenceforward they were
marked men. In Synods and Presbyteries, their general
teaching and their special utterances were keenly scrutinized.
Objections were put in the way of their transference to important parishes, and license was refused to young men who
were supposed to share their views. The Synod of Fife,
which included five of the twelve Representers, showed
special zeal in this direction, and actually ordered all its
members to sign the Confession of Faith again, with a new
clause,—'in view of recent decisions of the Assembly.' Ralph
Erskine for several years refused to comply, but in 1731 he
yielded, saving his conscience in a truly Scottish fashion by
appending the word 'allenarly' to his signature.[1] Ebenezer
steadfastly declined to do more than sign the Confession,
without the new clause, in the presence of his elders, in-
timating to the Synod that he had done so.[2] As the

[1] In Scots law allenarly is a restrictive term, equivalent to 'only'
or 'merely.' Ralph meant that his signature applied only to the
Confession, but he did not say so at the time.

[2] The strange fact came to light, that Ebenezer was one of five
members of his Presbytery who had not signed the Confession at their
ordination. The Presbytery, though startled by the discovery, attached no doctrinal significance to the omission, which, none the
less, illustrates the disorder of the Church.

strongest of the Marrowmen, he was called before the Synod repeatedly, and charged with unsound teaching, and, in defence, he for the first time published a number of sermons. Meanwhile several attempts to call him to vacant parishes were blocked by the Synod. Pamphlets were issued charging him with heresy and disloyalty. Matters went so far that, in 1727, he affixed to the Market Cross of Edinburgh a challenge to his anonymous slanderers to face him in the Assembly. The challenge, however, was not accepted, and about the same date the case expired in the Synod, no material having been found for the charges brought against him.

By this time the Assembly was again involved in doctrinal controversy. Rumours that Simson had not observed the caution enjoined upon him were, in 1726, shaped into a direct libel for specific Arianism, and during the progress of the libel he was suspended from teaching and preaching. Numbers of students were summoned as witnesses, and he himself was repeatedly examined by commissions and committees. But there was no laying hold of him or ascertaining his opinions. He showed some scattered learning and some acuteness, and again evaded the issue, having no enthusiasm for his opinions, nor any of the solid qualities needed by pioneers in theology. He disavowed some of the views with which he was charged, apologised for others, and declared, with sententious pathos, that he believed every word of the Confession of Faith. Yet it became perfectly clear that he had frequently denied, and even derided, the equal divinity of the Persons in the Godhead. Although the libel had other counts, this was its gravamen. Throughout the country, which was aflame with fiery literature, it was recognised that the Church's view of the divinity of Christ was in debate.[1] In 1728 the

[1] The keenest opponent of Simson was Principal Haddow, who was also a leading opponent of the Marrowmen.

Assembly resolved that Simson was 'now orthodox, but that he had taught and uttered false doctrine, and had given offence by not clearing himself when under trial, but deferred judgment for a year, transmitting all the documents[1] to Presbyteries for their opinion.' A majority of Presbyteries voted that Simson should be deposed, but in face of this vote the Assembly of 1729 agreed upon the lighter sentence of suspension, which would allow him to retain his status and his salary. Against this decision Boston of Ettrick protested, as 'derogatory to the supreme divinity of Christ.' The Erskines, who were present though not members of the court, were eager to adhere to the protest; but Boston, yielding to strong pressure, agreed that the protest should not be placed on record. Ebenezer in later life reproached himself for not having shown more firmness. The question at issue was, whether Simson should be maintained in a position which would enable him to go on propagating heresy, and the impression made by the decision, both in Scotland and in England, was that the Assembly, though willing on occasion to declare its own orthodoxy, was disposed to deal leniently with doctrinal deflections.

In this second phase of the Simson case the Erskines became more and more widely known as champions of evangelical doctrines. Ebenezer's sermons, especially those preached in Edinburgh, abounded in references to the divinity of Christ and to the freedom of the gospel.

'Oh invite others to come to the Tree of Life and to see that His fruit is good, pleasant, profitable and plenteous. Tell the hungry what excellent fruit is here; tell the weary what glorious rest is here; tell the diseased soul what healing leaves are here. Let your resentment run against those who would hew down the Tree of Life.

---

[1] *Processes against Simson* occupy 400 pages of close type. They are dreary reading, but those who have not read them ought to be cautious in generalising about the theology of the period. Scotsmen at their dullest have had a measure of discernment.

Oh stand up in His quarrel! Attempts have been made, even by some in our day and land, to cast Him down from His excellency; but sure I am, if you ever tasted of His fruit or were healed by His leaves, you will resent His quarrel and maintain His glory and vindicate His honour, against all the attacks that are made upon it. . . . Satan hath a party within this church, and the man that will stand on the Lord's side must resolve to have the world on his top. . . . One of the Lord's little ones may have a more clear and sound uptaking of the things of God than all the learned rabbis and plodding politicians in the world . . . Christianity is a fight; it is a battle, a hot battle; and there are not wanting some resolved to cleave to the standard. . . . There is a great cry for peace, peace, and many politic endeavours to keep the peace and unity of the Church; but it is impossible that we can be one, unless it be in the Lord. He is the centre of doctrine; there is not a word in the Bible but it points towards Christ, as the needle in the compass points to the pole star. He is the centre of worship; the prayers and praises of all believers terminate in Him.'[1]

Ralph was still keener and more constant in his contention. For ten years it was the prevailing theme of his facile pen. The best of his poems, *The Believer's Principles*, was composed as a popular exhibition of the debated doctrines, and in one of his published sermons he went as far as Ebenezer in forecasting trouble.

'Then is the Church in joyful circumstances when, by virtue of the gospel promise, children are brought forth to her. Such happy days have been in the Church of Scotland, when the spirit of reformation was poured out; but when that spirit is much quenched, and the gospel doctrine of free grace, which was the great instrument of conversion, is brought under much contempt and reproach, little wonder that God is like to give the mother-church a bill of divorce, that she be not the joyful mother of many children to Him. The free revelation of grace in Christ is the very womb of the Church, that brings forth her children; but nowadays the Gospel doctrine is brought under much disparagement—under much suspicion—as if it were some new dangerous scheme. . . . Such is the natural bias towards the Law as a covenant, and so natively does a church and people fall

---

[1] The sermon from which this is extracted was preached immediately after the Assembly had refused to depose Simson.

into it, even after and under a profession of sound principles, that, when evangelical doctrine comes to be revived in any measure, it is branded with novelty.'

He steadily maintained this conservative position, pleading for nothing beyond the assertion of Confessional truth. 'It is our mercy,' he wrote in 1725, 'that we have pure standards, and if any latter acts of this Church seem to clash therewith, I hope that they have not the deliberate approbation even of those that framed them. Much more do I entertain this charitable opinion regarding the rest of our Communion, that have not been engaged in the heat of those disputes.' Although as severe as Ebenezer in condemnation of the Assembly's decision, he was slower to see that the Church would acquiesce.

At an early stage in this controversy three young ministers, of whom we shall hear afterwards, gave in their adherence to the Marrowmen: William Wilson, Alexander Moncrieff and James Fisher. Wilson was the son of a Lanarkshire proprietor who had been outlawed for religion's sake under Charles II., and he had himself declined heirship to a wealthy uncle, tendered on condition of his becoming Episcopalian. He was a devout man, possessed of a well-balanced mind and powers of clear reasoning. The Presbytery of Glasgow refused to license him because of his scruples about the Abjuration Oath, but he betook himself to the Dunfermline Presbytery, in which Ralph Erskine secured him a friendly welcome, and in 1716 he was ordained as minister of Perth, where his piety and vigour soon made him the leading spirit in the community. Moncrieff, although also belonging to a family which had suffered for the Covenant, his grandfather having stood before the Privy Council with James Guthrie, was in comparative affluence, as the Laird of Culfargie, a pleasant and productive estate on the banks of the Earn. A scrupulously devout and conscientious man, with a turn for self-analysis, he was intensely conservative in his sympathies. 'Father hates everything new,' one of his children said, 'except the New Testament.' After graduating at St Andrews he had studied at Leyden under Marckius and Wesselius, and returned to Scotland with an eager zeal for evangelical orthodoxy. In 1720 he was ordained minister of the parish of Abernethy, in which his own property lay, and for nine years he exercised his ministry with quiet but anxious fidelity. From the first he was alarmed by the Simson case, but he stood somewhat aloof from the Representers, and it was not till 1729 that he publicly dissented from the policy of the Assembly. Fisher was a parish minister's son. Although a man of sound ability and high character, he had less distinctive quality. In his student days he was attracted by the Marrow doctrine, and frequented the Portmoak Church and Manse. Ordained in 1725 as minister of Kinclaven, he was married two years later to one of Ebenezer Erskine's daughters. At this stage he was the only one of the three who had any special relation to the Erskines. The minds of Wilson and Moncrieff were working in grooves of their own. Both of them were slow to abandon their loyalty to the Assembly, and there were scores of ministers throughout Scotland more likely, as things looked then, to break with the Established Church.

As those doctrinal discussions drew to a close, patrons, after a pause of ten years, began to claim their rights. Presentees ceased to be afraid to accept presentations without a call from the people, and when Presbyteries declined to ordain, patron or presentee appealed to the Assembly. In almost every appealed case, the Assembly instructed the Presbytery to proceed with the settlement. Sometimes Presbyteries obeyed, but in many cases they refused, having bound themselves by solemn resolution that they would ordain no man without a call. In this dilemma the Assembly betook itself, in 1729, to a contrivance which the warmest advocates of patronage have not ventured to justify. Instead of dealing directly with the inferior courts for disobedience, special committees were appointed to ordain the obnoxious presentees. Those committees were scornfully styled Riding Committees, partly because they over-rode the decisions of Presbyteries, partly because they moved on horseback from parish to parish on their unpopular errand. Haste was necessary. Sometimes church-doors were locked and barred against them; they could rarely find lodgings; and often they found themselves in personal danger from the indignation of the parishioners.

In almost every instance the ministers so ordained belonged to the laxer school of theology. The objection to their ordination was twofold—that they were not 'gospel ministers,' and that they had not received a call. The Marrowmen were strenuous in opposing forced settlements, and their views of the rights of the people developed rapidly. It became clear that the people wished to have an evangelical ministry, while patronage was habitually exercised in favour of its opponents. In 1727 Currie of Kinglassie issued a treatise *Jus Populi Divinum*, asserting with a novel precision the rights of church members to choose their own officials. A year later, Wilson of Perth wrote that 'disaffected heritors were introducing such ministers as elders and people were averse to—men who, neither in their doctrine nor in their walk, had any savour of Christ.' The development was rapid; the rationale of it may be debated, but the fact is indisputable. The cry, 'We have a right to hear the gospel,' was inextricably blended with the cry, 'We have a right to choose our own ministers.' In the Assembly the Neonomians supported the patrons, while in most Presbyteries the evangelicals asserted the rights of the people.

In 1730 the majority of the Assembly showed its mood by passing a resolution which deprived minorities of the cherished right of placing on record 'reasons for dissent.' In 1731 a far more momentous step was taken by the approval of an Act concerning the Planting of Vacant Churches. This Act declared that, in cases where the appointment to a vacancy devolved upon a Presbytery, the election should lie with 'the heritors, *being Protestant*, and the elders.' The persons so elected were to be proposed to congregations, who might, if they objected, state their objections to presbyteries, but in no circumstances were congregations allowed to call a minister. The Act had two stings. It prohibited Presbyteries, when appointments devolved upon them, from the prevailing and popular practice of entrusting congregations with the right of election, and it conferred that right upon heritors, as heritors, though many of them were Episcopalians and 'malignants.' In the settlement of 1690 and the Patronage Bill of 1712 there was neither precedent nor parallel to such legislation. Those had been Parliamentary enactments ; this was a voluntary surrender, by the Church, of rights which she had hitherto claimed. The Act came into force at once provisionally, and was transmitted to Presbyteries for their approval, in terms of the Barrier Act, which provided that constitutional changes could be made only with the consent of the 'plurality of Presbyteries.' During the year occupied by this procedure (May 1731—May 1732) the storm reached its height. It raged in every Presbytery, and was blown abroad by preachers and pamphleteers. Ralph Erskine was at the time absorbed in a local struggle for the rights of the Kinross parishioners, but Ebenezer's voice was heard at once in the Tron and Tolbooth Churches.

'The keepers of the walls had got themselves into that office for a piece of bread ; but instead of watching against the enemy, they

E

opened the gates. . . . What melancholy cries and complaints are going up to heaven, through several corners of the land, to the God of Sabaoth, the great King of Zion, against some set of men, who meet together in a judicative capacity, even in this city? I do not know but some of them may be hearing me. I shall only say that the injured little ones of Christ will have day about with those that carry it against them now. Before the whole scene be over, there will be wound for wound; tribulation will be rendered unto them that trouble the Spouse of Christ; and when the reckoning comes, the great men, and the mighty men, which are now adored, as if they were the only persons to be owned in the planting of churches, they, and those that join hands with them in conspiring to hurt the little ones of Christ, will be crying to the rocks and mountains to fall on them, and hide them from the face of the Lamb; when the poor people of God, that were accounted as the dross and the off-scourings of the earth, will be sitting upon the bench with Christ, everyone of them, shining forth like the sun in the Kingdom of their Father.'

Other preachers were as vehement, notably Currie of Kinglassie, who in a pamphlet designed to expose the crudities of the Act, took a still more threatening tone, declaring that the Assembly had created cause for a 'rent or schism' in the Church. In November, Moncrieff, Wilson and others drafted a Representation to the Assembly, craving that measures might be taken to check the growth and spread of error, intrusions into the ministry, and the procedure of the Assembly's committees. To this document the signatures of forty-two ministers and 1500 elders were affixed. It became clear that the Act would fail to gain the assent of Presbyteries; but a rumour spread that the Assembly intended to ignore this, and the excitement had become intense when the Assembly met. The rumour was justified by events. The Assembly, having indicated its temper by declining to hear the Representation, and by ordering the Dunfermline Presbytery to proceed with the disputed settlement at Kinross, went on to discuss the Act, although it had not secured the approval of the majority of the Presbyteries, and was therefore by church law annulled. Both of the Erskines took part in the discussion, their main contention being that the Act had 'no warrant from the Word of God, was inconsistent with the constitution of the Church, particularly with the Books of Discipline, and ignored the sole headship of Christ over the Church.' By a large majority, and in defiance of the Barrier Act, the Assembly approved of the Act, and declared it to be the law of the Church. Against this decision Ebenezer protested; but in accordance with the enactment of 1730 the Assembly refused to minute the protest. He went straight from Edinburgh to Stirling, and redelivered to his parishioners the substance of his Assembly speech, with some notable additions. He spoke of the universal Church, 'of which particular churches, national, parochial or domestic, are but branches,' as taking her constitution and her guidance from Christ alone, and proceeded to show that the Church has to deal with intestine enemies, corrupt officers, members and ministers, who pretend to build, yet cause the work to cease, so far as in them lies.' Against such enemies the true Church would prevail.

'Is it so that the government is laid upon His shoulders? Then see the nullity of all acts, laws and constitutions, that do not bear the stamp of Christ, and that are not consistent with the laws and orders He has left for the government of His Church. They cannot miss to be null, because Zion's King never touched them with His sceptre, and there is no church authority but what is derived from Him. . . . They run a very dangerous risk, who do injury to His subjects or strip them of any of the rights, privileges or immunities He hath granted them. Of these this is none of the least, that they should have the choice of their pastors. . . . They have a hard task to manage, who attempt to justle Him out of His government and take it upon their shoulders. . . . He will arise for the sighing of the poor and the cries of the needy; and oh, when He doth arise, the vengeance of His temple will fall heavy upon the heads of those who spoil it.'

Yet he concluded quietly, with words of consolation to

'the poor people of God when spoiled of their Christian liberty and privileges,' and by assuring them that 'He had power to provide them with honest ministers, notwithstanding all the bars that lay in the way of their being comfortably provided.'

In other districts there was far more violence in the protests that were raised, especially where the operation of the new Act at once showed its offensiveness. The Kelso Presbytery, for instance, ordained a minister, not only without a call, but without holding a regular meeting of the heritors and elders, in order that they might reckon the votes of certain non-resident heritors ; whereupon the whole district was thrown into a ferment.

When the Commission summoned the Dunfermline Presbytery to Edinburgh, in order to enforce the Kinross settlement, Ralph Erskine alone attended, and he positively refused obedience. Yet the Commission pressed on with its work. ' So up and down the land, the bride of Christ was outraged, the watchmen giving her away.' At the September meeting of the Fife Synod, Currie, when preaching as Moderator, broke out against the Act, calling it ' a direct crossing of Christ's institution and a robbing of His people'; but when he was called to account for his language, he published the sermon with some explanations, and the case ended. Indeed, everywhere it was uncertain how matters would shape themselves. Although the minority was large, it was not solid, and it had no definite plan, nor any scheme for united action. In Perthshire and Fifeshire, where it had its strongest representatives, it was supported by special sympathy. Yet even there the intensity of feeling varied. Some deplored the inroad upon the rights of the people ; others deplored the blow dealt at evangelical doctrine. There were only a few men upon whom both pressed with equal strength, and who felt that in both respects the Assembly had proved shamefully unfaithful. Even they had no idea of leaving the Church. Their one steady purpose was that, 'for Zion's sake, they would not hold their peace.' They had been silenced in the Assembly; but elsewhere, whatever it might cost, they would, in their favourite phrase, 'lift up the standard.' Yet no reader of these pages will doubt that the standard, once raised by a strong man, was bound to lead to victory or to be the signal for a division of the Church.

CHAPTER V

THE SECESSION

OF those who for twenty years had dissented from the policy of the General Assembly, Ebenezer Erskine was far the ablest and most vigorous man, and in 1732 he was the recognised representative of that party. There were two men who might have held a place beside him, Boston of Ettrick and Currie of Kinglassie; but Boston died in May, and in September Currie's courage failed him. In the Assembly indeed he had no following. The Marrowmen had died, or had betaken themselves to presbyterial and parochial affairs, leaving the Assembly to accelerate its course towards Moderatism. In Presbyteries and Sessions a party did exist, but as yet there had been no opportunity for measuring its strength and courage. Erskine had one great qualification to be the champion of a cause which in the Assembly seemed desperate, that he was by nature incapable of looking backwards to see how many were likely to follow him.

On October 10, 1732, it fell to him as Moderator to preach at the opening of the Synod of Perth and Stirling. Choosing as his text, 'The stone which the builders rejected, the same is made the headstone of the corner,' he preached a strong and stringent sermon upon the existing condition of the Church. He declared, without any circumlocution, that the builders of the Church of Scotland had for many years, with increasing disloyalty, been rejecting Christ. No Assembly since the Revolution had adequately asserted His Headship and Sovereignty. From

70

year to year alien influences had gained ground, and a general course of 'time-serving and peddling in politics' had culminated in an express abandonment of spiritual liberty. The Patronage Act was mischievous, but for that mischief the Church had not been responsible. Now the Assembly had of its own accord conferred upon heritors, who were not necessarily professing Christians, power to choose 'builders of God's house.'

'God's promise of guidance is given not to heritors or patrons, but to the Church, the body of Christ. As it is a natural privilege of every house or society of men to make the choice of its own servants or officers, so it is the privilege of the house of God in a particular manner. What a miserable bondage would it be reckoned for any family, to have stewards or servants imposed on them by strangers, who might give the children a stone for bread or a scorpion instead of a fish—poison instead of medicine! And shall we suppose that ever God granted a power to any set of men, patrons or heritors or whatever they be, to impose servants on His family without their consent, they being the freest society in the world!'

He pointed out that many of the heritors were disaffected to King George and to the Protestant Succession, and that they were bringing into parishes men who 'snuffed the light of Christ out of the Church with harangues and flourishes of morality'; men who, though they 'had got a smack of the learning in vogue, were utter strangers to the work of grace, and who took care to keep the power upon their side by bringing in none but men of their own stamp and spirit.'

'How are the rights of the Lord's people invaded and trode upon by violent settlements up and down the land! A cry is gone up into heaven against the builders. A complaint came before the last Assembly, for relief and redress of these and many other grievances; but, instead of a due regard had thereto, a new wound is given to the prerogative of Christ and the privileges of His subjects. . . . Whatever Church authority may be in this Act, it wants the authority of the Son of God. All Church authority is derived from Him, and therefore any Act that wants His authority has no authority at all. And seeing the reverend Synod has put me in this place, where I am in Christ's stead, I must be allowed to say that by this Act the Corner-stone is receded from, He is rejected in His poor members, and the rich of this world are put in their room. . . . Were Christ here present, I think He would say, "Inasmuch as ye did it unto one of the least of these, ye did it unto Me." I can find no warrant from the word of God to confer the spiritual privileges of His house upon the rich beyond the poor ; whereas, by this Act, the man with the gold ring and gay clothing is preferred unto the man with the vile raiment and poor attire. I judge it inconsistent with the principles and prac-tices of the best Reformed Churches, asserted in their Confessions of Faith, and particularly with the known principles of this Church, asserted in our Books of Discipline, which we are bound by solemn covenant to maintain.'

He closed by urging the Synod to ordain none to the ministry save those who showed acquaintance with the power of godliness, to 'stop these passages into the house of God, by which thieves and robbers most ordinarily enter, and to beware of being swayed in the matters of Christ with the favour of great men.'

'Let us watch the signs of the times, and whenever we discern the danger acoming, either from open enemies or pretended friends, let us give the cry like faithful watchmen ; and though fellow-builders be offended, there is no help for that. It is a heavy charge laid by God against some, that they were dumb dogs that could not bark, but pre-ferred their own carnal ease unto the safety of the Church.'

Erskine well knew that he would give offence, but a single sentence of the sermon proves that he was far from thinking of a secession.

'After all, I have good reason to believe that this Act is far from being the mind of the generality of presbyteries through this national church; and therefore I would gladly hope that a seasonable stand shall yet be made against it, in order to prevent its pernicious conse-quences.'

But men who are called 'dumb dogs' are apt to show

that they can not only bark but bite. When the Synod met, a prominent Moderate called attention to the sermon, and a keen debate followed. Erskine's reflections upon non-evangelical ministers, who despised the poor, had given as much offence as his condemnation of the Assembly and the obnoxious Act. The manuscript of the sermon was circulated, and he was called to explain certain selected passages. His defence was, that he had made no charges against individuals, that he was bound by vows of office to testify against error, and that the Confession of Faith distinctly recognises that, since 'Synods and Councils have erred and may err, their decisions are not to be made the rule of faith and practice.' When a vote was taken, it was decided, by a majority of six, that he 'was censurable for some indecorous expressions, tending to disquiet the peace of the Church and impugning certain Acts of the Assembly and proceedings of Church judicatories.' Accordingly, the Synod resolved to 'rebuke him and to admonish him to behave orderly for the future, and to appoint the Presbytery of Stirling to inquire into his after behaviour.' From the decision fourteen members of the court dissented.[1] As Erskine had by this time left, it was agreed that the rebuke should be administered at the April meeting of Synod. Against this he protested and appealed to the Assembly. In April he resisted urgent requests that he should withdraw his appeal, saying that, while he was sorry offence had been taken, it had not been shown that 'he had in the least receded from the Word of God and the approven standards of doctrine, worship, discipline, or government.' It is to be noted that the dissenters from the Synod's procedure, including Moncrieff and Fisher, did not profess to justify all Erskine's

[1] It is significant of the temper of the Synod that Fisher was disqualified from voting on the ground that Erskine was his father-in-law.

language; but declared their inability to accept the position that the Assembly's decisions were above criticism. His own appeal to the Assembly was respectful but firm. He pointed out that he had been censured without any particular charge being brought against him, and 'on the ground of a multitude of expressions in cumulo,' that he had broken none of the standards of the Church, and had only exercised a right to judge of the decisions of the Assembly, which was expressly guarded by the Confession of Faith. He acknowledged that there was 'a multitude of men in the Established Church with whom he was not worthy to be compared.' At the same time he renewed his protest against the Act of 1732, as a departure from Presbyterian principle, and ruinous to the Church.

When the Assembly of 1733 met, it declined to hear protests from Wilson, Moncrieff and Fisher. Erskine was represented by an advocate, who seems to have misunderstood the case. After hearing him, the Assembly confirmed the action of the Synod, 'found the expressions vented by Mr Erskine to be offensive and to tend to disturb the peace and good order of the Church, and appointed him to be rebuked and admonished by the Moderator in order to terminate the process, which was done accordingly.'

So runs the Assembly's minute, showing the desire of the Assembly to conclude the troublesome case. Erskine tendered a protest, countersigned by Wilson, Moncrieff and Fisher,[1] in which he stated that, although he had a 'great and dutiful regard to the Church judicatories, he held himself at liberty to preach the same truths of God and to testify against the same or like defections of the

[1] This was the first occasion on which the names of the Four Secession Fathers appeared together. Wilson humorously compared the four to Ezekiel's Living Creatures, Erskine being the man, Moncrieff the lion, Fisher the eagle, while he himself was satisfied to labour as an ox.

Church upon all proper occasions'; but the Assembly declined to receive the document, and the four protesters withdrew, leaving it upon the table. As providence ordained, however, the protest fell from the table, and was picked up by 'a certain fiery man in the corrupt measures of that time, who, having read it, called the Assembly to pause in the business to which they had proceeded, and to consider the insufferable insult committed upon them in the paper.' The Assembly listened, and 'appeared to be all in a flame.' They recalled the Four, and ordered them to withdraw the protest, but they refused. The Assembly decided that they should appear before the Commission in August, 'to express their sorrow for their conduct and misbehaviour in offering to protest.' In the event of their refusing, the Commission was instructed to suspend them from the ministry, and thereafter, at the ordinary meeting of Commission in November, to 'proceed to a higher censure.' The Four returned to their parishes and quietly resumed their duties, with the unbroken and enthusiastic support of their parishioners. In August, they declared to the Commission their adherence to the standards of the Church of Scotland, asserted their liberty to protest against any erroneous decision of the Assembly, and intimated that they would regard as intruders any who might be appointed to their parishes. At the same time the Stirling Presbytery, which had been instructed by the Assembly to take notice of Erskine's conduct and behaviour, reported thus: 'His character is so established among the body of professors, in this part of the Church, that we believe even the authority of the Assembly condemning him cannot lessen it: yea, the condemnation itself in the present case will tend to heighten it.'

The Commission, in accordance with the Assembly's instructions, suspended the Four from the ministry. They paid no heed to the suspension, save by taking counsel together as to how they should proceed if, in November, the Commission took a further step. In a sermon preached at Queensferry on August 12, Erskine showed his firm purpose, by speaking of a 'rising storm which would make all to stagger,' and by enforcing the duty of maintaining the 'liberties and privileges of the Church, handed down by the blood of Christ and the blood of many martyrs.' Among many traditions of his apposite use of the Psalms, it is said that he prefaced this sermon by giving out these two verses:—

> My closed lips, O Lord, by Thee
> Let them be opened ;
> Then shall Thy praises by my mouth
> Abroad be published.
>
> Shew kindness and do good, O Lord,
> To Zion Thine own hill ;
> The walls of Thy Jerusalem
> Build up of Thy good-will.

Meanwhile petitions without number reached the Commission, earnestly deprecating further action against men whose character and work were irreproachable, and against whom no charge had been laid. The provost and magistrates of Stirling declared that they had 'found Mr Erskine to be a man of most peaceable disposition.' The Perth municipality said that Wilson's ministrations had been of inestimable benefit to the religion and morality of the town. No fewer than sixteen synods requested the Commission to pause, saying that 'a great and open breach,' 'a total separation and schism,' would be the result of imperious action. Those representations had so much effect that, in November, the Commission was in great perplexity. By the casting vote of the Moderator it was resolved, in compliance with the Assembly's instructions, to proceed to a higher censure ; but, when this was resolved, attempts were made to effect a compromise. The Four were en-

treated to withdraw their protest, on the understanding that
the Commission would recommend the following Assembly
to declare that the liberty of ministers was unimpaired;
but, after deliberation, the Four replied that they could
not evade the plain fact that the Assembly had 'restrained
their ministerial freedom and faithfulness, and that their
protest against this restraint must stand.'

Accordingly, on November 16, the Commission resolved
'To loose the relation of Mr Erskine, Mr Wilson, Mr Moncrieff, and Mr Fisher from their respective charges, to declare
them no longer members of this Church, to prohibit all
ministers to employ them in any ministerial function, and
to declare their charges vacant.' This was qualified by a
declaration that, 'in case they should behave themselves
dutifully and submissively, and should make appeal to the
meeting in March next, the Commission would then recommend them for favour to the next Assembly.'

The Four, however, had their own ideas of dutiful
conduct. When the sentence was passed, they read
the following document :—

'We hereby adhere to the protestation formerly entered before this
Court, both at their last meeting in August, and when we appeared
first before this meeting. And further, we do protest in our own
name, and in the name of all and everyone in our respective congregations adhering to us, that, notwithstanding of this sentence passed
against us, our pastoral relation shall be held and reputed firm and
valid. And likewise we protest that, notwithstanding of our being
cast out from ministerial communion with the Established Church
of Scotland, we still hold communion with all and everyone who
desire, with us, to adhere to the principles of the true, presbyterian,
covenanted Church of Scotland, in her doctrine, worship, government and discipline; and particularly with those who are groaning
under the evils, and affected with the grievances we have been
complaining of, and who are, in their several spheres, wrestling
against the same. But, in regard that the prevailing party in this
Established Church, who have now cast us out from ministerial
communion with them, are carrying on a course of defection from

our reformed and covenanted principles, and particularly are suppressing ministerial freedom and faithfulness in testifying against the present backslidings of the Church, and inflicting censures upon ministers for witnessing, by protestations and otherwise, against the same: therefore we do, for these and many other weighty reasons, to be laid open in due time, protest that WE ARE OBLIGED TO MAKE A SECESSION FROM THEM, and that we can have no ministerial communion with them, till they see their sins and mistakes, and amend them. And in like manner we do protest, that it shall be lawful and warrantable for us to exercise the keys of doctrine, discipline and government, according to the Word of God, the Confession of Faith, and the principles and constitutions of the covenanted Church of Scotland, as if no such censure had been passed upon us, upon all which we take instruments. And we hereby appeal unto the FIRST FREE, FAITHFUL AND REFORMING GENERAL ASSEMBLY OF THE CHURCH OF SCOTLAND.

'EBENEZER ERSKINE.
'WILLIAM WILSON.
'ALEXR. MONCRIEFF.
'JAMES FISHER.'

Seven other ministers, including Ralph Erskine and Currie, tabled a protest, in which they declared their intention to hold communion with the Four in spite of the Commission's sentence, and claimed for themselves the liberty of speech for which their brethren had been condemned. But their protest did not involve them in the Secession, and for three years the Four, and they alone, were known as Seceders. The designation, which they themselves had chosen, had a recognised meaning. Turretin and other eminent theologians had contended that, at the Reformation, Protestants had not incurred the guilt of schism, but had 'seceded' from the Romanised majority. Secession was thus a *vox signata*, indicating the right and duty of a minority, when overborne, censured, and silenced, to maintain a separate Church life, in fidelity to Church principles, and without any severance from the life of the true Church. This was the position which Ebenezer and his three allies took. The 'prevailing party' having refused to hold communion with them, they responded by refusing to hold communion with the prevailing party. They seceded from that party, as not representing the true Church of Scotland, with the belief that their secession would be vindicated when Scotland again had an Assembly free, faithful, and reforming. While their Secession was not designed to be final, they from the first meant it to be definite, and recognised that the causes which had led to it were deep rooted. It had no incidental or personal basis. The statements and documents which they issued were measured and explicit, without any trace of resentment or pique. They had resolved to continue their testimony for truth and freedom, and their resolution was of the steady and unswerving kind which church authorities have always failed to baffle.

Their temper and intention are placed beyond dispute by their immediate action. They appealed neither to Church courts, nor to the people, but agreed to meet in three weeks for prayer and conference, as knowing that every step they took must be measured and devout. The meeting-place selected was a roadside hamlet, Gairney Bridge, three miles from Kinross, chosen partly as central between their four parishes, and partly for its seclusion. Some legends say that they met in an inn, others that they met in a stable, but it is more likely that they met in the schoolhouse.[1] They were within a stone-throw of the parish to which Erskine had ministered for thirty years, and their thoughts were burdened by the severance of inherited ties which their own zealous labours had strengthened. The first day was given to prayer, humiliation, and frank conference. On the second day, December 6, 1733 :—

[1] In 1883 a monument was erected on the spot, the dedication address being given by Principal Cairns on December 5, 150 years after the date of the meeting.

'After much and serious reasoning on both sides of the question, they did all, with one voice, give it as their judgment that they should presently *constitute into a presbytery*, and the Rev. Ebenezer Erskine was, by their unanimous consent, desired to be their mouth to the Lord in this solemn action, and he was enabled, with much enlargement of soul, to consecrate and dedicate them to the Lord, and to the service of His Church, particularly of His broken and oppressed heritage, in the situation into which by the holy and wise providence of God they were brought, and after prayer he was chosen Moderator of the Presbytery.'

The surroundings of the scene were plain, perhaps meagre. Yet the engravings of it, which represent four grave and courtly dignitaries, met in solemn conclave, truly reflect the importance of the step that had been taken. By forming a Presbytery they gave a permanence to their work which no amount of ecclesiastical contention or of demagogic oratory would have secured. They laid the foundation of a Church, national in its ideal, conservative in its creed, and orderly in its procedure, even when casting off parliamentary influences and asserting the rights of conscience. The interested stranger who discovers, in the twentieth century, that nonconformists in Scotland differ, in their ideas and in their attitude, from nonconformists in other countries, and that half of the Scottish people are included in a Church without Statutory position, yet as national in spirit, and as strictly presbyterian, as the Established Church, will take the first step to understand the situation when he goes back to Gairney Bridge, and notes the spirit in which Ebenezer Erskine, William Wilson, Alexander Moncrieff and James Fisher, after constituting themselves into a Presbytery, 'did refrain from proceeding to acts of jurisdiction till they should see whether the courts of the Church would return to their duty.'

Their first business was to issue a precise and full explanation of the step which they had taken, and of the reasons which had influenced them, for they were 'standard-bearers,' and the legend on their standard must be distinct. Within three months, they published a Testimony to the Doctrine, Worship, Government and Discipline of the Church of Scotland—a searching review of the policy of the Assembly since the Revolution, in its bearing upon the Headship of Christ, and upon the preaching of the doctrines of grace. It is difficult to get at the original form of this document, which, in later controversies, was republished, with amendments, by some who wished to exaggerate, and by others who wished to minimise, the quarrel of the Seceders with the Established Church.[1] Yet it is only in the original that the truth is exactly told. The Testimony declares that they have formed themselves under God into a Church court, in order that they may be in a condition and capacity to exercise all the parts of their pastoral office, with enjoyment of the blessings promised by Christ to His faithful Church; in order that they may maintain proper order, distinguishing themselves from 'those of the sectarian and independent way,' and be in a better capacity for affording help and relief to the oppressed heritage of God through the land; and in order that they may lift up more than a personal testimony against the present declinings and backslidings from Scotland's Covenanted Reformation. It proceeds to charge the prevailing party with breaking down 'our beautiful Presbyterian Constitution,' with pursuing measures which corrupted the doctrine of the Confession of Faith, and with carrying on its evil courses with a high hand, so that the Seceders were not suffered to protest 'in a way of ministerial communion.' Hitherto they had contended and wrestled within the Church; but now the current of defection ran with such an impetuous torrent that they must secede from communion with the present prevailing party, till they were

[1] It is doubtful if any edition printed after 1736 is trustworthy.

F

sensible of their sins and mistakes, and reformed and amended the same. In their enumeration of the Assembly's offences, an impartial reader cannot say that either more or less weight is attached to doctrinal decisions than to the intrusion of ministers. The general charge is that the Assembly, by continued unfaithfulness to the sole sovereignty of Christ, has fostered an unfaithful ministry, and deprived the people of their right to the blessings of gospel preaching. The Testimony anticipates the charge of schism, and deals with it frankly. The Seceders had not left the Church; they had been thrust out; but besides, schism being in its essence a 'departure from Church order and unity,' the blame for the Secession rested wholly upon those who were breaking down 'the order and unity to which Scotland was bound by solemn covenant.' Again and again the Testimony disavows 'sectarianism and independency, which lodges the keys of government in the whole community of the faithful, and refuses the subordination of the congregational elder- ship to superior judicatories.' Again and again it asserts that the Secession is made, not from the Church of Scot- land, but from the prevailing party in the Established Church. Yet those cautious limitations only serve to emphasise the impression left by the Testimony as a whole, that the roots of the Secession, as of all per- manent movements in the Church, were deep set in history.

About themselves personally, their sacrifices, risks, or probable losses, the Seceders said not a word. They had no thought of organisation, and made no provision for the future. Each of them separately had commended wife and children to God ; but they had been born and trained in homes familiar with greater sufferings for religion's sake than could possibly be their portion. For Henry Erskine's son, to swerve through fear of poverty was impossible, and his three comrades had similar guidance from the past. The real strain laid upon them was the severance which they had been led to make, and the pressure of that strain was severe. In their private diaries and correspondence a sense of wistful regret and uneasy reluctance is disclosed. Yet this found no public expression, and surely their silence will be approved. When men are driven by conscience to take a step which will probably bring them and their children to poverty, which will sever their outward connection with the Church for which their fathers laid down life, and which nine out of ten of their neighbours will condemn, they show true courage by refraining from lamentations and pathetic requests for sympathy. They were genuine in their prayer that the prevailing party would alter its ways. Three of the four, being comparatively young men, cherished a definite hope that the prayer might soon be fulfilled. It is scarcely possible to ascribe such a hope to Ebenezer Erskine. He was in his 54th year, and he knew the Church which he left.

CHAPTER VI

RIDING THE MARCHES

THE 'prevailing party' was startled and perplexed by the attitude and the procedure of the Seceders. Their position, as defined in their Testimony, was clear and firm. They claimed for the people the right to a voice in the appointment of ministers. They protested against unevangelical teaching. They condemned the Assembly for enforcing the settlement of ministers to whom parishioners objected, and particularly for entrusting Church duties to secular persons. They declared their intention to protest against those departures from the principles of the Church, not merely as individuals, but as an orderly Court of the Church of Christ. The facts to which their Testimony pointed were patent, and created general sympathy with them, especially in those parts of Scotland where their personal character was best known. Yet the sympathy was vague, and the Secession might have terminated, if the Assembly had either persisted in its policy or retraced its steps. There was, however, no leadership in either of those directions. For six years the Assembly evaded the points at issue, prevaricated, generalised, talked about concessions, but conceded nothing; while the roots of the Secession were spreading, without any deliberate effort on the part of the Seceders. Apart from the merits of the case, the proceedings of those six years give a remarkable example of ecclesiastical blundering.

When the Assembly met in May 1734, it revoked the

84

Acts of 1730 and 1732, and declared, 'to prevent mis-apprehensions and for the satisfaction of all, that due and regular ministerial freedom was still left entire to all ministers, and that the same was not, nor should be held or understood to be, anywise impaired or restrained by the late Assembly's decision in the process against Mr Erskine.' An Act was further passed empowering the Synod of Perth to restore the Seceders to the Communion of the Established Church, and to their parishes, but forbidding the Synod to express any judgment upon former procedure in the affair. In terms of this Act, the Synod at a meeting held in July removed the suspension, and 'reponed' the Seceders in their parishes. The Stirling Presbytery promptly showed its cordial concurrence by appointing Erskine its Moderator.

Thus the Seceders were again acknowledged by the Established Church as her ministers, and for five years their title to that position was not challenged in the Church Courts. It lay with themselves to recognise the Courts of the Church and take part in their proceedings, or to refuse to do so,[1] and their decision was not reached without hesitation and some temporary division of opinion. In January 1735 Erskine wrote courteously to the Stirling Presbytery declining the proffered Moderatorship.

'There is a difference to be made betwixt the Established Church of Scotland, and the Church of Christ in Scotland; for I reckon that the last is in a great measure driven into the wilderness by the first. And since God in His adorable providence has led us into the wilderness with her, I judge it our duty to tarry with her for a while there, and to prefer her afflictions to all the advantages of a legal establishment, in communion with judicatories as they stand at present. And this, I firmly reckon, is no schism before the Lord, whatever it may be reckoned in the eyes of the world. Whenever it shall appear to me that the established judicatories are heartily adopting the cause of

---

[1] In technical language this was described as 'acceding to the Church Judicatories,' accession being the reversal of secession.

Christ, purging and planting His house, according to His will and the solemn covenants lying upon the land, and giving justice to His oppressed members through Scotland, I hope not only to return to communion, but to enter the gates of our Zion with praise.'

Three months later, Erskine's view was emphasised and defined in a joint-statement entitled 'Reasons for not acceding to the Established Church,' in which the Seceders pointed out that the Assembly's sentence against them had not been rescinded, but only abated for the sake of peace, and that they had received no guarantee for the liberty of speech which they had claimed. Without such guarantee, they dared not furl their standard. They could return, they said, with clear conscience, only if the Assembly would (1) assert the supreme divinity of Jesus Christ and proceed against all who denied that doctrine; (2) specifically rescind the Acts of 1733; (3) declare that, in spite of patrons' legal rights, no ministers should henceforward be ordained without the consent of congregations; (4) authorise the dispensation of ordinances to parishioners burdened by 'intruded' ministers; (5) take new measures to enforce evangelical preaching; (6) appoint a national fast for the acknowledgment of past defections. Those claims were sweeping, yet Moncrieff and Wilson thought that the Assembly might comply with them; and, as long as this seemed possible, the Seceders refrained from all acts of separatism. Ebenezer dissuaded a former parishioner, who consulted him, from deserting the ministrations of an intruded presentee. They busied themselves with their parish work, presiding over their Sessions, administering the sacraments, assisting as in former days at neighbouring communions, but absenting themselves from meetings of Assembly, Synod and Presbytery. When invitations reached them from neglected parishes to institute new congregations, they refused, saying that they had 'not clearness to act judicially.' Their so-called presbytery-meetings were mainly devotional in character, and were often held in the manses of ministers who, though not Seceders, were in sympathy with the Secession cause.

In 1736, the aspect of affairs was changed, and the Secession passed into a new phase. Ebenezer had always feared that the desire of the Assembly to preserve peace implied no willingness to make a change in policy, and in that year his fears were fully justified. The Assembly, while passing some resolutions designed to propitiate the Seceders, dealt leniently with the first full-fledged Moderate who had to answer at the bar for heresy—Professor Campbell, the author of a pamphlet with a sufficiently descriptive title, 'The Apostles no Enthusiasts.' A vague declaration as to the rights of the people was discounted by instructions given to Presbyteries, to proceed to induct several presentees in the faces of unwilling parishioners. In fact a new hand was at the helm. Archibald, Lord Ilay, had found an able henchman in an Edinburgh professor, Dr Patrick Cumming, and it was recognised that the days of compromise were near an end. At this crisis the Erastianism which appointed the Porteous Act to be read in churches, created a new scandal, and awakened dissatisfaction with the relation between Church and State in parishes which had been untouched by the Secession. Before the year closed, the Seceders set aside their hesitations and issued a Judicial Testimony, as an intimation to Scotland that they were ready to discharge all ecclesiastical functions. This Testimony, in which the Erskines concurred, although they had no share in the drafting of it, came short of the previous one both in tone and in breadth. With many provincialisms and bigotries, after the manner of the times, it included protests against the Union of the Kingdoms, and the repeal of the laws against witchcraft. Its chief interest is that, while it deepened the lines of the First Testimony, it showed some progress of thought in regard to the relation between Church and State. For the first time in Scotland, the principle was asserted, that 'the enforcing of religious duties with civil penalties, and in too many cases blending the affairs of Church and State with one another, is inconsistent with the spiritual nature of Christ's kingdom.' Yet the principle was undeveloped, and in another passage wistful reference was made to the time when the true religion was authorised by laws and acts of parliament.

While issuing this manifesto, the Seceders, now of one mind, set themselves to meet the requests for gospel ministrations which poured in upon them. Within twelve months, requests came from seventy or eighty parishes, chiefly through Praying Societies. As they still numbered only four, and had the full duties of their ministry to discharge, they had to leave scores of requests unfulfilled. But they appointed Wilson as 'professor,' and entrusted him with the training of candidates for the ministry. Meanwhile a single visit went far to establish a Secession congregation in an 'oppressed' parish. On such visits they preached two or three sermons in succession—their sermons were far shorter than those of the Moderates— saying little about the Secession specifically, but insisting upon the headship of Christ, and the freedom of the gospel. They baptised children, ordained elders, and dispensed the Lord's Supper. They assured their hearers that as soon as possible ordinances would be regularly supplied, and advised them for the present to attend the nearest parish church in which there was a gospel ministry. In some cases the ministers of neighbouring parishes countenanced them, and attended their services. In other cases they had to face angry opposition and threats of violence. Tales lingered, for a hundred years, of occasions when mobs, armed with pitchforks and stones, gathered with the intention of preventing worship, and were awed into shame by the fearless dignity of the Erskines. That those tales were not mere legends, may be seen by an extract from the *Caledonian Mercury* of March 22, 1738, to which equally authentic testimony might be added.

'A grand convention was held yesterday of the adherents to the seceding ministers of the Church of Scotland, in a square plain on Braid Hills, two miles south of Edinburgh. About 10 before noon, the minister of Orwell opened the service with a sermon. At noon Mr Wilson, one of the ministers of Perth, preached and afterwards baptised ten children, brought thither, some 20, some 30 miles off. At four afternoon, Mr Ralph Erskine, one of the ministers of Dunfermline, preached. The apparent tendency of these sermons was to excite fervour and devotion and a renewal of solemn engagements, to deprecate sin in general, and those of this corrupt age in particular,[1] and it was observed that it is not proper or expedient (either to wash away sin or to indemnify the sinner), to purchase indulgence at the hand of the kirk-treasurer, and some other tenets that savoured of a popish tincture were soundly lashed. There were about 5000 hearers at each sermon (I mean of the household of faith) besides the ungodly audience, consisting of many thousands, some of whom set fire to furze ; others hunted the hare around 'em to create disturbance, a certain huntsman having had a plot to carry off the collection.'

This extract shows that the Seceders had gained a weighty addition to their ranks. In the Secession itself Ralph Erskine took no part. Although in 1733 he was one of those who protested against the decision of the Commission which deposed the Four, three years passed before he 'gained clearness' to cast in his lot with them. He was present as a spectator at the Gairney Bridge meeting, and approved generally of the procedure; he frequently preached in the Seceders' churches, and invited them to his own pulpit; several of their early meetings were held in his manse. Yet he could not bring himself to join them definitely. It was not exactly want of courage that hindered him, although

---

[1] At this point the writer has caught the tone of Pliny's letter to Trajan describing early Christianity.

he certainly shrank from exposing his children to the risk of poverty, and showed an anxiety as to the views of his parishioners, of which the others gave no sign. His conservative sentiments clung more closely to the outward fabric of the Church of Scotland, and he feared the development of democratic tendencies. Early in 1733 he wrote to a friend :—

'I see we stand just now in a dangerous post, and yet in a middle place—between the kirk and the people, so to speak ; the kirk, that would drive us to popery, making the judgment of ministers, simply, to constitute the relation between a pastor and people, and so lording it over their consciences by obtruding ministers upon them without their consent ; and the people, many of whom would, at the roots, drive us to independency.'

Although he struggled stoutly against the intrusion at Kinross, and had incurred the direct censure of the Assembly for his firmness, he cherished the feeling that it was enough to protest and dissent, until his evangelical zeal was roused by the Assembly's dealing with Professor Campbell. In 1735 and 1736, he spoke against Campbell's heresies in the Supreme Court, and when, in the latter year, it was resolved only to caution the offender, he recognised that a new situation had arisen. His diary shows that the decision which he now reached had for four years been the theme of meditation, prayer and fasting.

'Oct. 16, 1732.—I got liberty to pray over parts of Scripture read, and to express confidence in God . . . with reference to His countenance of my brother in his present circumstances, that integrity and uprightness may preserve him, with sweetness of frame and high expressions of humble confidence in the Lord.

'Nov. 7, 1732.—Having read some Scriptures, I was helped in prayer, and my heart was melted and poured out in view of God as a promising God. After I had acknowledged my corruption and confusion, I was made to grip to God's word of promise in all my ministerial work. And I had in view my attending the Commission ;

and, acknowledging my utter unfitness for doing anything, prayed that He would pity and be present with me. . . . I went to Edinburgh, the affair being our refusal to receive and enrol Mr Stark as minister of Kinross. I was alone, no other minister of the Presbytery being there.

'1733.—Endeavoured a confession of my heart-sin and nature-sin, my sins of practice in childhood, youth and riper age, laying principally upon the greatest sore and owning unbelief and atheism. I was led to put my right hand and right eye sin into the hand of Christ, that He might break the same. Then I arose and considered the covenant of promise.

'May 3, 1733.—After reading several Scriptures, my heart was much sweetened and enlarged, and my hope through God in Christ strengthened. After this, I went to the Assembly, where I and my brethren had a great battle, with reference to our having refused to receive Mr Stark.

'Dec. 5, 1733.—I went with Ebenezer to the Bridge of Gairney, where he and his three brethren spent all day in prayer and conference. There was, I thought, much of the Lord with them, and I found my heart frequently warmed and drawn out in prayer with them.

'1734 (?).—It was put into my mind to appoint a family fast, and I had in view deliverance from mine own sinfulness. Accordingly I called all my family together that were capable, and spent the whole forenoon in praying, singing, and reading, intermixing confession and supplication. I thought the best inheritance I could leave the lass and the five lads was God Himself.

'1736.—I wondered at the office I am called to, acknowledging that they should be angels and holy persons that are witnesses for Him; yet declaring before God that I thought it was some regard to His great name that swayed me in going out to this business.'

In August, he handed to the Commission, 'with much sinful fear and perplexity,' a paper declaring his adherence to the Testimony; but the Commission refused to receive the paper. In October, he and Thomas Mair of Orwell, another minister who was moving in the same direction, spent some days at Culfargie Manse, 'reasoning with the four brethren about the present situation.' This was followed by a long diet of prayer and fasting with the Dunfermline Presbytery, in which both ministers were 'greatly beloved.'[1] At this stage Ralph's inward struggle was intense. His diary is a strange comment upon those partisan histories which represent him as leaving the Established Church in a reckless and cankered mood.

'Jan. 6, 1737.—I heard Mr Mair give in reasons for his secession from this Church, and his accession to the brethren. Whereupon afterwards my mind was asked, and I owned myself to be yet unclear—that I was taking it under consideration.

'Jan. 8.—I set aside a part of this day for prayer. I was thoughtful about that great business of secession, and sought the Lord would give me light.

'Jan. 18.—I wrote to Mr Mair my thoughts, and laid down some arguments and reasons that weighed with me against a present secession.

'Jan. 29.—I had many struggles in my mind, and wrote a letter to Mr Mair concerning my scruples, who having sent my line to Messrs Wilson and Moncrieff, they wrote letters, which to me were weighty, and induced me to a farther consideration.

'Feb. 14.—Mr Mair came, and was fully resolved to make a direct, absolute sort of secession. I was not his length. . . . We prayed together. I was helped, and had my heart poured out in acting of faith, looking to the Lord for conduct and fleeing to Jesus for pardon. Also, this morning, Isaiah xliii. and xliv., last part of former and first part of latter chapter, were refreshing to me and matter of pleasant meditation, somewhat encouraging in the present work. I was at this time much in darkness and confusion, yet desiring to follow all the light and freedom I had, namely, to join the brethren in their adherence to the Testimony, and to disjoin from the judicatories of the Church, so far as my joining with the former made joining with the latter inconsistent.'

---

[1] Many examples of his conspicuous devoutness were quoted in parish manses. It is told that, when the Presbytery was hearing students' exercises, he was called to give his judgment on a 'trial-discourse.' 'What is that, Moderator?' he said; 'I forgot it was upon trials. I was hearing for the edification of my soul.'

On the date of the last entry he invited his elders to confer and pray with him on the subject, and ascertained that they were 'generally against the deed, fearing the issue'; but, anxious as he was to secure their support, his own mind was now clear.[1] On February 16, he handed to the Dunfermline Presbytery a Declaration of Secession from the present judicatories, and two days later his name was added to the roll of the Secession Presbytery. In the Declaration, he was careful to define his intentions and ideas, saying that he had embraced no new views, and desired to contend for the very truths which he had steadily, though ineffectually, maintained throughout his ministry, 'bearing witness for the cause of Christ and His truths, against the defections of this Church and land.'

'The four brethren being particularly stirred up to this work by a remarkable chain of providences, I think myself obliged to join with them in this matter; not as they are a presbytery or a judicatory separate from the Church of Scotland, but as they are a part of that same Church, constituting themselves, in the Lord's name, as a judicatory of ministers associating together, distinct from the present judicatories, and witnessing against their corruptions and defections; insomuch that, by withdrawing from these judicatories at present, and joining with the said brethren, I intend and understand no withdrawing from ministerial communion with any of the godly ministers of this national Church, that are groaning under, or wrestling against, the defections of the times, even though they have not the same light with us in every particular contained in the foresaid Testimony. Nor do I hereby intend to preclude myself from the liberty of returning to and joining with the judicatories of this Church, upon their returning to their duty, and so far as my joining with the foresaid, or any other ministers, in their lifting up the said Testimony, and promoting the end and design thereof, and the said return can consist together; seeing, if the judicatories, who at present either unjustly refuse or

---

[1] Hill Burton suggests that the Seceders were urged into the Secession by their elders. There is not a hint of this in the documents which he quotes as his authorities for the period.

unduly delay to receive that Testimony, were acting a contrary part, and putting hand to reformation, the same reasons that induce to this withdrawing, would necessarily induce to a returning, which I cordially wish I may quickly see good reason for.

'And though I am sensible what a bad tendency division natively has, and desire to abhor and shun all divisive principles and practices, contrary to the doctrine, worship, government and discipline of the Church of Scotland, agreeable to, and founded upon, the Word of God, and judge it my duty to endeavour, through grace, to follow after that peace that has truth for the ground and ornament of it ; yet the safest way for pursuing peace being to cleave unto Jesus Christ, who is the centre of all true and holy union, and to advance the truth as it is in Him, I therefore think myself obliged, leaving events to the Lord, to take the present opportunity of joining with other brethren in what I reckon a faithful testimony.'

The reluctance with which Ralph had proceeded, and the reserve of this Declaration, increased rather than impaired the value of his accession to the cause. His resolute and skilful advocacy of evangelical truth was known far beyond Scotland, by men who cared little for Acts of Assembly or disputes about patronage, and in Scotland it was recognised that his notably devout attachment to the Church had been broken by the pressure of strong conviction.

At this stage the Seceders required such support, for the uncertainty of their relations to the Established Church rapidly passed into direct antagonism. It became plain that, though they might still reckon themselves ministers of the Church of Scotland, their methods must result in the rise and the organisation of a separate Church. Many who had up to this point shown sympathy with them began to condemn them. Men reputed for piety and orthodoxy, like Willison of Dundee, who had hitherto given them inexpensive assistance by inviting them to Communions and sending them intimate expressions of good-will, were now sorry that the 'standard' had been lifted out of the Assembly and planted on open ground. It is almost comical to read the reproaches which they levelled at the Seceders, for they themselves had not for years lifted a finger publicly in the cause of truth and liberty. Yet the sincerity of their sorrow is unquestionable, and they were obviously unable to continue in Communion with the Seceders. Although in some cases personal friendliness was maintained, ministerial intercourse ended, and with this a new element of hardness appeared in the preaching of the Seceders, especially of Ebenezer Erskine. It is true that he refused to advise his hearers to absent themselves from their parish churches. Yet when he found that the faces of his old allies were set against him, he was led into broader censures of the ministers of the Established Church than he had previously expressed, and with these there were blended occasionally references to faint-hearted men who had failed in the day of battle.

It was not, however, his words that gave provocation, his chief strictures being passed upon tavern-haunting ministers, and preachers of Arian, Arminian, and Socinian doctrine. It was the fact that the Secession Presbytery now formed kirk sessions, and administered sacraments, thereby ignoring the discipline of the Established Church. As yet, they ordained no ministers,[1] but it was known that an increasing number of candidates were studying at the Perth Manse, and that they would be ordained as soon as they were fully trained.

In their own parishes both of the brothers had perplexities. Ralph's Session, although at first opposed to Secession, soon followed him, and on December 15, 1737, after a diet of fasting, formally adopted the

[1] John Hunter, the first minister ordained by the Secession Presbytery, was ordained at Gateshaw on October 17, 1739; he had received the first part of his training in the Established Church.

Testimony; but his colleague, Wardlaw, was one of those evangelicals who disapproved of the Secession, and about this date the difference made its way into the pulpit. Ralph's diary shows how he tried to avoid strife :—

'Feb. 22, 1737.—This evening I talked with Mr W. in a friendly way about the peace and concord we should study, declaring I had made no secession from him, and that we ought to abstain from every word that would seem to import any difference in public between him and me; to which he assented. And I found him and the people generally more easy than I had feared.

'Feb. 27, 1737.—I lectured forenoon, and gave a note concerning people joining with the builders, whether in the inside or the outside of the wall, in order to caution the congregation against leaving my colleague.

'May 7, 1738.—Afternoon my colleague fell upon the Secession before his close, alleging that, though the defection in Israel was universal, yet Caleb and Joshua went not out from them, and that we were to wait upon God, who had other ways of delivering His Church than some thought of. This was very uneasy to me, and obliged me in the evening exercise to say something on that subject. This was a trial I did not just now expect, after some former exercise and assistance the Lord afforded. No doubt matters are coming to an extremity in the Church. May the Lord pity, help, and guide, and mercifully over-rule!

'Dec. 1738.—My circumstances with my colleague are trying; he differing from our way of testifying, and some leaving him, and his crying out against them.'

The difficulty, it will be noted, was that the Dunfermline people wished to leave Wardlaw. Ralph and the Session strove to prevent this, which would involve an open rupture, and for two years—till 1739—they succeeded, yet only by caution and self-control.

Ebenezer's difficulties, on the other hand, were with his Session, his colleague Hamilton being one of the few non-seceding ministers who were unswerving in support of the Seceders. In 1736, five of his elders began to absent themselves from session meetings and from church, on the ground that Erskine was no longer a minister. Hamilton rebuked them publicly, and he and Erskine, with the support of the majority of the session, intimated that they would remove from the church-roll those who were 'ignorant of the first principles of religion, hostile to the distinguishing tenets of the Church of Scotland, negligent of secret and family worship, habitually absent from church and from catechising, or ungodly or immoral in life.' The five elders, taking offence at this, appealed to the Assembly, which decreed that they were the only Session of Stirling. The five accordingly made claim to the church-door collections, in which claim they were supported by the Burgh Magistrates. One of the interesting points in the controversy, which dragged on for two years with a good deal of pettiness, was that it led Erskine to formulate the principle that all congregational office-bearers must be elected by communicants at open meetings. As interesting, though less satisfactory, was an outbreak into which he was led when the five elders appeared at the church-door and appropriated the collections. He read from the pulpit a formal protest against their intrusion, as 'a robbery and rape, committed upon this congregation, contrary to the liberties with which Christ had made them free.'

'And I, for my further exoneration, as a messenger and herald of the great King, whose name is the Lord of Hosts, do in His name, summon the following pretended and intruded elders, Henry Christie, William Maben, Robert Banks, Andrew Millar, and Henry Allan, who have broken the comely order of the house of God in this place; and all others, whether in ecclesiastic or civil authority, who have aided, abetted, and countenanced them in this their wickedness and iniquity, to compear before the bar of Christ, the King and Head of His Church, at the time He hath in sovereignty appointed, to answer for their conduct. I do also, by the same authority as above, warn all in this congregation under my inspection, to beware of countenancing or owning the above-mentioned men as lawful officers in the church of Christ, as they would not partake of their sin and punishment.'

G

This is the only recorded occasion on which he completely lost his balance, and fell into unworthy personalities. Without justifying him, one must admit that the Assembly had created a position for him in which a reasonable line of action could scarcely be maintained. While deliberately asserting that he was minister of the parish of Stirling, the Supreme Court had declared that the session over which he presided was not the kirk-session of Stirling, and had given that title to men who refused to acknowledge his ministry. One entry in his diary gives still clearer proof of the incongruity of the position.

'May 20, 1738.—I preached on Revel. i. 7 before the Judges on circuit, my Lords Dun and Strichen. I had not had time to write, having just returned from the Associate Presbytery at Abbotshall.'

Thus, while taking part in the work of a dissenting church court, he was recognised by law as a parish minister.

By this time, however, the end of the ambiguity was within sight. At the beginning of 1738, complaints against the 'disorderly practices' of the Seceders began to take shape in presbyteries and synods. The ministers of Abbotshall and Burntisland, Thomas Nairn and James Thomson, had adopted the Testimony, and rumours were abroad of still more important secessions. In May, the Assembly condemned the Seceders, now eight in number, as schismatics, and instructed the Commission to prepare and execute a libel, but at the same time declared its preference for a meek, brotherly and forbearing method. Ministers were further enjoined 'to endeavour by conference, and other gentle means of persuasion, to reduce and reclaim the brethren to their duty and to the communion of the Church, and to seek to recall the poor deluded people, who had been carried away by the discussion.' When in pursuance of this injunction some well-meaning ministers proposed a conference, the Seceders responded that they were ready to meet with them as fellow-christians, but that, as a Presbytery, they could confer only with an official body. In November, the Commission resolved by a narrow majority to issue a libel, and in March each of the eight was summoned to appear before the Assembly, ' to answer for unwarrantable secession, and persistence in secession ; for erecting themselves into a Presbytery ; for publishing as a Testimony certain calumnies against the Church ; for ordaining elders and dispensing sacraments outside the bounds of their own parishes.' In accordance with Church law, the libel quoted instances of those offences, and in Ebenezer Erskine's case the sermon preached against his five rebellious elders was specially named.

While the libel was being drafted, two semi-official publications served to popularise the contention, to harden it, and to give it permanence. A pamphlet on Separatism was issued, with the approval of the Assembly, by John Currie of Kinglassie. For twenty years Currie had been Ebenezer's intimate friend. He had given thanks with him in the Portmoak Manse, on the day of his conversion. They had contended together, as co-presbyters, against Erastianism and for the Marrow doctrine. Currie had gone further than Erskine in asserting the divine right of the people. He had warned the Assembly that, if the four brethren were deposed, the Assembly would be to blame for a deep and lasting rent in the Church. He had protested against their suspension, and declared his intention to hold communion with them in defiance of the Assembly. Then, in November 1733, he drops out of sight, until in 1738 he re-appears—the author of a stringent denunciation of the Seceders, as guilty of unjustifiable schism. The pamphlet itself supplies no explanation of this change of front, and it is to Ebenezer's credit that he steadily refrained from those personal retorts, to which a man of smaller mind would have resorted. Yet when here and there a sharp, sad word escapes him about 'those who have deserted us in the evil day,' or 'the familiar friends who have lifted up their heel against us,' he has, no doubt, in mind this once trusted ally.

The reply to Currie, which was entrusted to Wilson of Perth, appeared in 1739, as a 'Defence of the Reformation Principles of the Church of Scotland.' Although the Erskines were not, even in part, the authors of the Defence, their lives are unintelligible without some acquaintance with it. It was the recognised apology for the Secession, having been revised by Fisher and Moncrieff, and it represents, with precision and fulness, that view of the relation between Church and State which both Ebenezer and Ralph habitually asserted.

The general argument of the Defence is, that the Secession was justified by the public and flagrant failure of the Established Church to maintain the historical principles of the Church of Scotland. Wilson was too learned a man to assert that the absolute right of congregations to elect their ministers was a Presbyterian principle, but he had no difficulty in proving that the Church of the Reformation had claimed that there must, at some stage, be a 'call,' indicating the assent of congregations. He disavows the view that the civil magistrate has no right to meddle with religion, and acknowledges that the legal establishment of religion is good in itself, and may be serviceable to the Church. But, he says, legal establishment has become a snare, and has subjected the Church to irreligious influences, so that outward communion with her has become a hindrance to the discharge of duty. The civil bond, created and maintained by parliaments, is not the true bond of the Church. Her unity is spiritual. It is one thing to depart from a particular provincial or national church, on account of its corruptions, and another thing to separate from the Catholic visible Church. The National Church, as represented by the present judicatories, has not the Scriptural character of a Church of the living God. Since she does not maintain the standards, she cannot be said to hold them. Loyalty to the Headship of Christ, and care for the edification of His body, zeal for the purity of His institutions, and for the liberty He has given His people, must be the chief concern of office-bearers; and to maintain 'a profane syncretism or coalition with the enemies of these,' for the value of a civil bond, is unjustifiable. Therefore, the Church of the Secession is not distinct from the Church of Scotland, but a living part of it. If separation is thus justifiable, the maintenance of separate ordinances needs no separate defence; for sacraments and ordinances are designed to maintain Christian life, and are in no way dependent upon Acts of Parliament or other civil agreements. The Seceders have a threefold right and duty to dispense ordinances; (1) as ministers of the Catholic Church; (2) through their particular relation to the national and visible Church of Scotland; (3) as bound by the Confession of Faith to aid, support, and assist one another in the defence of Reformation rights, principles, privileges and liberties.

When those views were published, they seemed bold, presumptuous, and destructive; but whatever the reader's ideas of Church unity may be, he will recognise that, except in the Roman Church, they have since steadily gained ground throughout western Christendom.

When the Assembly of 1739 met, there was divergence of opinion, resulting in a keen debate. Some contended for summary discipline, arguing that the Secession was already losing its force, and that it would collapse before vigorous treatment, like the factions headed by M'Millan, Hepburn and Taylor. Others maintained that conciliatory measures alone would prevent a 'spreading wound,' and this view was supported by a special plea from the Irvine Presbytery, that the Assembly should pause in a course which threatened to have dismal effects, in driving the 'peaceable and orderly into schism.' After two days' debate, the Assembly, by a narrow majority, resolved to proceed with the libel and to summon the Seceders to the bar. When they appeared, the Moderator informed them that ' notwithstanding all that was passed, the Assembly was willing to receive them with open arms if they would return into the bosom of the Church, and to let all bygones be bygones.' In response they stated, through *their* Moderator, that they had come as a Presbytery, constituted in the name of the Lord Jesus Christ; and they presented an Act and Declinature, in which they declared that 'the present judicatories were not lawful, nor right constitute Courts of Christ, and declined all authority, power and jurisdiction of the said Courts.' The Declinature, which was a lengthy document, closed with an appeal which seemed audacious :—

' The Presbytery deem it their duty, with all humility, tenderness and earnestness, in the bowels of our Lord Jesus Christ, to entreat and beseech their reverend, worthy and dear brethren who regard the covenanted testimony of the Church of Scotland, and desire to be found faithful to the Lord, to come out from all ministerial communion with the present judicatures in regard they were constitute, as said is, of such corrupt and scandalous members . . . for the sake of the weary, broken and scattered heritage of God through the land ; as also, that they may be in a capacity to transmit a faithful testimony to succeeding generations. . . . As for this Presbytery, whatever the conduct of the judicatures towards them may be, and however they may be borne down, reproached, and despised, they are persuaded the cause is the Lord's; and however weak and unworthy they are, whom He hath singled out in His adorable providence to put hand to a testimony for Him, and whatever He may see meet to do with them, they desire to rest in faith and hope, that the Lord will build up His Jerusalem in Scotland, and gather His dispersed Israel into one.'

Having read this document, they returned to their own

place of meeting, and, 'having seriously considered the direction and assistance which, they hoped, the Lord had been pleased to give them, in their essay at this time of testifying in the above manner,' they concluded their meeting with thanksgiving and prayer.

To the hasty reader this punctilious formality will perhaps seem grandiose and pretentious; but it has a different aspect to those who consider the permanence and the growth of the Church, which thus deliberately detached itself from the control of the Assembly. It was not through formalism or pride that they refused to deal with personal charges, or to lay their foundation upon minutiæ of procedure. They had resolved to raise a platform from which they and their successors could speak to the people of Scotland.

When they withdrew, some members of Assembly scoffed, but the majority recognised the gravity of the situation, and a resolution was passed declaring that, though the offenders deserved to be deposed, sentence should not be pronounced upon them for another year, 'in order to give them a further time to return to their duty, and to render them still more inexcusable if they should persist in their unwarrantable separation.' At the same time a Committee was appointed to draw up a statement of the whole case for publication. A year brought no change, except the increase of Secession, and the development of the plans of the Seceders. In May 1740, the Assembly resumed consideration of the case, and, seeing that the accused made no appearance in defence, found, by 140 to 30 votes, that the libel was relevant, and proven, deposed them from the office of the holy ministry, declared their parishes vacant, gave instructions for the immediate appointment of successors, and sent copies of the sentence to the Magistrates of the burghs concerned.[1]

---

[1] Colonel John Erskine, who had preserved his affectionate regard for Ralph, was one of 19 members who dissented from this finding.

It is significant that the Moderator, in his closing sermon, combined a violent attack upon the 'divisive practices and the pretended sanctity' of the deposed ministers, with a protest against the 'hard law and grievance of patronage'; such was the anxiety to nullify the claims of the Seceders.

This was the termination of the case, which, in its different phases, had occupied the Assembly for seven years; but in the minutes of 1741 there is an entry which cannot be overlooked:

'The orders of the late Commission for £60 to Mr John Currie, minister at Kinglassie, for his writings published in vindication of this Church, were approven.'

CHAPTER VII

THE ERSKINES AS SECESSION MINISTERS

THE parochial work of the Erskines was very slightly affected by the sentence passed upon them by the Assembly. In the long course of the proceedings, their parishioners had been familiarised with the idea of separation from the Established Church, and, having resolved to follow their ministers, were ready to face the emergency. Indeed the only change made was in their places of worship.

At Stirling,[1] on the Sunday following the deposition, the magistrates forbade the ringing of the church bells, and barred the church door. The people assembled at the hour of worship, determined to force an entrance ; but Erskine dissuaded them from violence. Raising the pulpit Bible, which, according to the custom of the day, he had brought with him from his house, he protested before God that he was not responsible for the events of the past week, and led the way into a neighbouring field, where he preached an uncontroversial sermon, on the power of Christ to control the winds and waves. He showed his wish to continue the historical line of witness-bearing, by choosing his text from the passage on which Guthrie had preached, when leaving Stirling to die. Within a few months a large church was built, and there, for the rest of his life, he ministered to a greatly increased congregation, his own parishioners being augmented by bands of Seceders from neighbouring parishes. On

[1] Erskine's colleague, Hamilton, had died in 1738.

December 31, two delegates from the Presbytery took formal possession of the old church, but they found no worshippers. For seventy-seven years the church was left empty. In spite of the Assembly, Erskine remained the real minister of the parish. When, in 1745, Government wished to communicate with the people of Stirling, it was to Erskine that they wrote.

Ralph's experience at Dunfermline was different. As early as 1739, when the Assembly first served a libel upon him, his congregation built a church to hold 2000 people,[1] in which he conducted worship at one service, while continuing to preach at the other service in the parish church. Wardlaw, his colleague, being an opponent of the Secession, an attempt was made to maintain an 'interdependent position'; but, when a choice was forced upon the congregation, they almost unanimously resolved to leave the Established Church. They did not require to leave in haste. Until 1742, neither magistrates nor Presbytery interfered, and Ralph retained his position of 'interdependence'—a position which was consistent with his contention that he had not left, and would not leave the Church of Scotland. His quaint view is clearly expressed, in a sermon preached immediately after his deposition, on the text, 'The Lord gave, and the Lord hath taken away.'

'The ministerial office is what the Lord gives; and I may say, even to me, who am less than the least of all saints, is this grace given. As He gave me this grace, this office, so He has from time to time given me some seals of my ministry, both here and elsewhere. And as it is God the Lord that gives, it is also the Lord only that can take away.

---

[1] The elders, he writes, have gone through the parish for subscriptions. . . . It is expected that at least £400 will be gathered even among the poorer sort, for the most part. . . . The collection is so universal that it is surprising both to friends and to enemies. What am I, that such favour should be expressed towards me in this place? Great and marvellous are Thy works, Lord God Almighty!

. . . I dare not, at the will and pleasure of man, cast away what He gave; and since He yet gives me opportunity of opening my mouth in His name, I embrace it as His continued gift. When the blessed apostles were deposed from the ministry, and forbidden to speak any more in the name of Jesus, they declared that they would obey God rather than men, and accordingly taught and preached in the Temple as long as God restrained the outward violence of men.'

At the same time he braced his parishioners for the coming change, with an earnestness that passed sometimes into threatening.

'If you continue to make choice of me for your minister, I judge it is only God's immediate hand that can loose the relation betwixt us. If my heart deceive me not, I would rather choose to suffer with you—to live on bread and water—than to have any active hand in separating what God has joined; and I design, as the Lord shall give health and ability and liberty, to prosecute my ministry among you in the name and strength of the Lord. But if any sinful sentence of men shall tempt you to despise and disparage my ministerial office and work, you must answer for it before His awful tribunal, where you must have some other thing than the authority of any Assembly to bear you out.'

Such appeals, being supported by fervent preaching, in which the sole authority of Christ over Church and over conscience was the dominant theme, and by frequent diets of congregational prayer and fasting, appointed by the Session, were, for the time, almost completely successful. In 1742 he could say publicly: 'I know not of seven or eight persons, among all the 8000 examinable people of this parish, but seem to be still satisfied to subject themselves to my ministry in peace.'

This situation might have continued indefinitely, had not the Assembly expressly enjoined the magistrates to perform their duty, and appealed for support to the Secretary of State and the Lord Advocate. At this crisis Wardlaw died, and the Presbytery, driven at last to action, declared both charges vacant, and appointed one of their number to take possession of the church. Although Ralph cautioned his congregation to behave peaceably, 'as its being the Lord's Day,' there was a slight riot, which has been vividly described by a spectator.

'May 11, 1742.—This afternoon Mr Hardy of Culross being appointed to take possession of Mr Erskine's pulpit, whose diet it was this Sabbath, the Established party came a little after the second bell, and caused lock the porch door, as the ministers always entered the east door. Mr Erskine's congregation were mostly without, in the church-yard. The east door was guarded by David Black of Hill, Bailie Chalmers, Bailie John Walker, and others, to keep out Mr Erskine. But when he came through the church-yard with Mr Brisson, many following, as they came near the east kirk-door, Mr Brisson cried out, "Make way for your minister." Upon this, some rushed in ; others, that were within, soon turned back the gentlemen door-keepers ; neither could they get the door shut, so that when Mr Erskine came forward, none of his opposers had power or courage to make the least resistance against him ; his presence struck a terror in them. The way to the pulpit was lined on every side, so that Mr Erskine had a full and free entry to it. During all this time, Mr Hardy was in the session-house trembling, for he would not mount the pulpit till he saw that Mr Erskine was kept out of the kirk, and, when the small scuffle was at the kirk-door, he called to lock the session door, and when the kirk was composed and the psalms singing, he went forth with his gentlemen door-keepers to Bailie John Walker's house.'

At this stage Ralph withdrew from the struggle. Yet he published three Solemn Admonitions, warning his parishioners that, if they took part in the calling of another minister, they would incur the wrath of God. Their guilt, he said, would be the deeper, because he was not only their lawful minister, but 'a public witness for the persecuted cause and truth of Christ.' His greater intensity in controversy, to which reference has already been made, made him less masterly and effective than his brother in management. Of his twenty-six elders and deacons, a bare majority finally adhered to the Secession, five continuing in the Established Church, and seven claiming to be neutral. Two efficient ministers were settled in the vacant parish, and the empty church was gradually filled. Yet Ralph's new church was crowded, and he continued to be the chief man in the community.

The Erskines were so much affected by the general fortunes of the Secession that notice must be taken of the experience of their associates after deposition.[1] Fisher preached without interruption at Kinclaven till August 1741, and even then the law was brought into operation, only when he had accepted a call to become the first Secession minister at Glasgow. Moncrieff's strong position as a wealthy laird prevented any forcible interference with his ministry; but he voluntarily closed the Abernethy church, and preached in the churchyard till he had built a new place of worship. He refused to take any stipend from the congregation, and indeed partially endowed the new church. Wilson's experience closely resembled Ebenezer Erskine's. On the Sunday after his deposition, Perth was in an uproar. It was known that the magistrates had barred the church-door. One of Wilson's domestic servants, who had passed through the Bloody Days in his father's service, said to him as he left the manse: 'Tak' tent, Master William, tak' tent. If things gang on this way, I'll get yer meat to carry to the muir, as I did yir guid father's afore ye.' When he reached the church, he demanded admission, in the name of Jesus Christ. Two contending crowds had already begun the use of stones and staves, but Wilson stepped between them, saying: 'No violence, I implore you: I serve the King of

[1] The word Associate gained at this time an ecclesiastical meaning. The Seceders styled their Presbytery the 'Associate Presbytery,' a designation which became historical, although it had no particular propriety.

Peace.' He led the way to the Glovers' Yard, which had been tendered to him by the Corporation, and there preached, on the words, 'Let us go forth therefore unto Him without the camp, bearing His reproach.' While a church was being built for him, he preached weekly in the open air. The exposure told upon his health, and to the great loss of the Secession cause, as will be seen presently, he died within eighteen months of his deposition. Until his death, however, he furnished another illustration of the rule, that the Seceders retained a strong, if not an exclusive, hold of their parishioners.

Meantime the Associate Presbytery had to deal with urgent requests for 'supply of sermon.' Propagandism, even if there had been a disposition towards it, was out of the question. Many requests could not be met for years. They refused to ordain anyone who had not been as fully trained as the law of the Church of Scotland required, and, until the number of their probationers increased, they could arrange for worship in clamant parishes only every sixth or eighth Sunday. Baptism was, as a rule, administered on week-days, and every baptism was prefaced by a sermon to which neighbours were invited. The evangelical attractiveness of those baptismal services laid the foundation of nearly half of the Secession congregations —an interesting parallel to the progress of many understaffed Foreign Missions in modern times. In some cases kirk-sessions acceded in a body, and maintained ordinances as presbyters, with sessional authority. In other cases Praying Societies took the arrangements in hand, and held devotional meetings when there was no regular service. So, in spite of limitations and obstacles, the Seceders multiplied. In 1742 there were twenty Secession ministers and thirty-six organised congregations; and in 1745 they had so increased that they found it necessary to form three Presbyteries—Edinburgh, Glasgow, and Dunfermline—which met half-yearly as a Synod.

Their work was mainly evangelistic. When they visited parishes, they appeared, not as ecclesiastical partisans, but as preachers of gospel truths ignored in the Established Church. They preached nowhere without invitation, and invitations rarely, if ever, reached them from parishes where the ministers were evangelical. Like the Church which, a century later, gave up civil establishment for the sake of freedom, they gained hold of the people by preaching the gospel. While this assured their progress in Scotland, it secured adherents elsewhere. In England, where Presbyterians were moving towards unitarianism, Secession congregations were formed, here and there, by those who could not check the movement and would not yield to it, and in Ireland there was a similar result, through the prevalence of Arianism. By men who were neither Presbyterians nor Scots, it was recognised that this was their dominant note and motive. As early as 1739, George Whitefield wrote of Ralph Erskine as 'a field-preacher of the Scots Church, a noble soldier of Jesus Christ, a burning and shining light who had appeared in the midnight of the Church'; and, in 1741, Ebenezer wrote to Whitefield :—

'The wandering sheep come with their bleatings to the Associate Presbytery, whereby our work is daily increased. . . . We must feed and rally our Master's flock, scattered and offended by the Established Church.'

In accordance with this purpose, they made it their first business, as a Presbytery, to draft and issue an 'Act concerning the Doctrine of Grace.' The Act, which was prepared by Ebenezer Erskine and Moncrieff, and adopted in 1742, contains no doctrinal novelties, and is only a clear assertion of those Confessional truths which the Assembly had disparaged in recent controversies. Its effectiveness is shown by the fact that, in 1744, the Assembly found cause to issue Instructions to Sessions, 'touching some aspersions cast upon this Church, as if she had given up with all the fundamental doctrines of Christianity.'

The preaching of the Erskines at this period was in line with the teaching of the Act—concise, uncontroversial, and catholic in its tone, and their pastoral work was at its very best. Their personal dignity, which had social as well as moral elements, and was partly inherited, became conspicuous, and prevented any decrease of their influence through the new relation in which they stood to their congregations. Without any priestliness, they naturally maintained their official position, and were uninfluenced by the fact that they now depended for their living upon voluntary contributions. There are some grounds for believing that their stipends were as large as formerly, but this is a vague inference. Financial affairs were not obtruded upon them, and are never mentioned in Church records, in their journals, or in their private correspondence. There is one exception. When preaching ordination sermons, they insisted, with Pauline frankness, upon the claim of the husbandman to partake of the fruits, and they declined to ordain ministers unless there was adequate provision for their maintenance.[1] For many years the Secession Church had no funds or schemes of any sort. Its one professor had no salary.

They maintained, without wavering, the idea that they were ministers of the Church of Scotland, with national rights and duties. It would have been well for them, and for those who came after them, if they had confined this idea to their personal affairs and their parishes. The introduction of it into Church courts was full of mischief. As early as 1741, in accordance with their extreme conservatism, it was proposed to renew the Solemn

---

[1] Their idea of adequacy was, in the case of country ministers, about £60 per annum. This was higher than the legal minimum stipend of parish ministers, which in 1750 was £44, 8s. 10½d. ; but the early Seceders had neither manses nor glebes.

League and Covenant. In 1743 fifteen ministers took the Covenant at Stirling, and in 1744 Covenanting was declared by the Presbytery to be a term of communion, although one to be 'applied with tenderness and lenity to the weak of the flock.' The taking of the Covenant was in itself a harmless piece of religious antiquarianism; but, as taken by men who had enunciated a broad principle of religious liberty, it was an inconsistency so glaring that it could not but lead to confusion. Covenanting rested upon the theory that the civil powers are entitled to support as defenders of religion. Indeed the Covenants plainly assert that 'the only true religion . . . must be received, believed, and defended by the King and the Estates, as God's eternal truth,' and that Covenanters are bound 'to discover to the civil powers those who hinder reformation, for their condign punishment.' One of the Seceders, Nairn of Abbotshall, raised objection to the revival of the practice, alleging that it was worse than absurd to combine an oath to uproot Episcopacy with an oath of allegiance to a monarch who had sworn to uphold Episcopacy. The Presbytery evaded the issue, by saying that their allegiance to the civil powers extended only to civil matters, and that they renewed the Covenants 'in a way suited to their circumstances.' Nairn, who certainly had logic on his side, dissented and seceded[1]; and the Presbytery thought they ended the matter by repeating, that 'the civil magistrate had no lordship over conscience, that it was not suitable to blend civil and ecclesiastical matters in the present situation, and that they themselves were not in favour of propagating religion by offensive arms.' They refused to 'impugn a Government which, though uncovenanted, allowed the free exercise of religion, and did not unhinge the liberties of the Church.' Yet the controversy set some

[1] Nairn's logic was sound; but he was inconsistent. He ultimately made his way back to the Established Church. See M'Kerrow, i. 330.

H

of the younger men athinking and the compromise was short-lived.

The continued respect of the Erskines for the civil powers, and their special zeal for the House of Hanover, were tested and proved by the Rebellion of 1745. Ebenezer organised a corps of volunteers at Stirling, and acted, not as chaplain, but as captain. It is told that when Stirling was in danger from the Highland Host he appeared in the guardroom in uniform. The officers on guard tried to persuade him that his vocation and his years unfitted him for active service. He replied: 'I am determined to take the hazards of this night, for the present crisis requires the arms as well as the prayers of all good subjects.' The most notable proof of his loyalty is that the Marquis of Lothian, who had been Royal Commissioner to the very Assembly which deposed the Seceders, earnestly requested him to appoint Lord Robert Kerr, his son, as colonel of the Secession corps, which had stipulated for leave to nominate its own officers, and that the offer was willingly accepted. In his correspondence with Lord and Lady Lothian, which, from the first word to the last, bears the stamp of gentle and dignified courtesy, Ebenezer professed his extreme pleasure in co-operating with a family which had 'made such appearances for the Protestant interest, and our reformation-work in Scotland.'

'In this your noble family and we, who are Seceders from the Established Church, do happily agree; for our secession from the present judicatories goes purely and only upon this very ground, that we think they have, in many particulars, departed from the covenanted doctrine, discipline, and government of the Reformation Church of Scotland.'

When the rebels occupied Stirling, he for a time filled a twofold office, preaching to his congregation in the woods of Tullibody on Sundays, and leading the volunteers on week-days in movements which again and again brought him into danger of life. Ralph was not less loyal, though his loyalty was less severely tested, and the young Seceders were in no respect behindhand. While Moncrieff's estate was plundered and his children were carried off by the rebels, Ralph's son, Henry, who was by this time settled as Secession minister at Falkirk, headed the volunteers of that town, and in recognition of his services was created an honorary burgess of Glasgow. Some lines from a curious poem of Ralph's on 'The Civil Magistrate' show the stage their thoughts had reached:—

'To Civil Powers let great regard be given,
And human laws that cross not those of heaven.

.   .   .   .   .   .

Apostles order all their flocks and ours,
For heavenly ends to stoop to earthly powers;
Nor for their want of qualities divine
Must we their just authority decline.'[1]

With this fervent loyalty, they maintained their view with regard to the relations between Church and State. Ralph's dictum, in the above lines, that the civil powers have a want of 'quality divine' may seem to have behind it the theory that 'the State should deal only with the public good of outward and common order.' Yet neither he nor Ebenezer so held that theory as to shake their belief that the State should suppress religious error, and support Reformation principles. It is true that official Secession documents of this period contain, in absurdly close proximity, two inconsistent views: (1) that the State has neglected its duty to espouse and support the Covenanted Church; (2) that the State has nothing to do directly

[1] In *The Social Life of Scotland* the Seceders are described as absorbed in trivial disputes, while Established Church ministers were displaying loyalty. The contrast has no foundation in fact. In September, 1745, *e.g.*, when the Insurgents marched south, the Seceders suspended debate and, under Adam Gib, assisted actively in defence of Edinburgh. Hill Burton recognises their 'marked zeal.'

with the Church. But the former of those views, alone, is found in the writings of the Erskines. Both brothers were disinclined to assert a new theory. It is true that, in Ebenezer's sermons of this period, there are several significant retrospects of history. Reviewing the 180 years of the life of the Reformed Church, he shows that, for more than half of that period, the Church had the State as her enemy, and that her noble days were days of independent struggle for truth and freedom. He speaks as if he were confirming, by his own experience, the truths he had learnt in boyhood at his father's death-bed, and had accepted the idea that the bond between Church and State is a purely secular one, which must always hinder the work of the Church. Yet time after time he sets aside that thought, and recalls 'real visitations of God's spirit, when the true religion was authorised by Acts and Laws of Parliament.' He is satisfied with demonstrating that the actual influence of the State upon the Established Church is injurious, and that the Assembly, by its backsliding, has forfeited all claim to represent the Church of Christ in Scotland. Upon this he, like Ralph, insists with increasing vigour. 'The present judicatories,' he says, 'will give way, when the nail of legal sanctity, upon which they depend, is removed.' Once he goes so far as to declare that 'no true-born child of God will herden with robbers and thieves.'

Their antagonism to the Established Church was one, though not the only, cause of a complete change in their relations to George Whitefield, and of their hostility to the local revivals which followed his visit to Scotland in 1741. When Whitefield's Calvinism involved him in contention with the Wesleys, he looked to Scotland for sympathy, and began an intimate and affectionate correspondence with the Erskines, especially with Ralph, who wrote to him as father to son, guiding him in choice of books and other matters. The correspondence resulted in a proposal, which they afterwards ascribed to him, and he to them, that he should visit Scotland, partly in order to evangelise, and partly in order that he might 'sit at the feet of the Associate Presbytery, and be taught the way of God more perfectly.' Those were his own words ; but the Erskines asked him to go further, and to undertake that when in Scotland he would follow their guidance. They were specially anxious that he should revise his views of Church government, and were convinced that they could persuade him to disavow Episcopacy. They had also, though in a minor degree, some anxiety lest he should 'strengthen the enemy,' by preaching in the pulpits of the Moderates. Whitefield refused to come under any pledge, declaring that he meant to remain neutral as to Church government, and to preach to all who were willing to hear him. This reply perplexed the Associate Presbytery, and letters were sent to him hinting that his visit might do more harm than good. The Erskines scarcely shared this apprehension, and when he arrived at Leith, in July 1741, Ralph welcomed him cordially at the wharf. He had, however, as a rival welcomer, the Rev. Alexander Webster, Ebenezer's brother-in-law, one of the strangest products of the Scottish Church. Webster was an extremely popular evangelical minister, and at the same time the most jovial of boon companions. 'No one in Edinburgh could joke with him ; no one could drink with him ; when all others were drunk, he was perfectly sober ; and this boon companionship lessened in no degree the high estimation in which he was held.'[1] Withal he was a statistician and the founder of the Widows' Fund, one of the best schemes of the Established Church. At this crisis he showed a wisdom, which was none the less politic because it was in line with his convictions, by preventing

[1] Cunningham's 'Church History of Scotland,' ii. 319 ; Morren's 'Annals,' ii. 376. In one of those features at least he was Socratic.

Whitefield from identifying himself with the Secession cause. At first he failed. Ralph managed, as he wrote to Ebenezer, to take Whitefield, 'over the belly of vast opposition,' to Dunfermline, where he preached to Ralph's congregation and secured his warm approval. Ralph wrote at once to his brother as follows :—

'I had conversation with him alone to-day. About his ordination, he owned he then knew no other way, but said he would not have it that way again for a thousand worlds. As to his preaching, he declares he can refuse no call to preach Christ, whoever gives it ; were it a Jesuit priest or a Mahometan, he would embrace it, for testifying against them. He preached in my meeting-house this afternoon ; the Lord is evidently with him.'

Whitefield's account of their intercourse is equally cordial.

'Mr Ralph received me very lovingly, and I preached to a very thronged assembly. After I had done prayer and named my text, the rustling made by opening the Bibles all at once quite surprised me : a scene I never was witness to before. Our conversation after sermon in the house was such as became the Gospel of Christ.'

Ralph escorted him back to Edinburgh, where he preached to a crowd in the Orphan-house Park.

'After sermon, a large company, among whom were some of the nobility, came to salute me. Amid our conversation, came in a portly, well-looking Quaker, nephew to Messrs Erskine, who, taking me by the hand, said, "Friend George, I am as thou art ; I am for bringing all to the life and power of the ever-living God ; and therefore, if thou wilt not quarrel with me about my hat, I will not quarrel with thee about thy gown." In this respect, I wish all of every denomination were thus minded.'

So far, Ralph seemed to be of the same mind as his Quaker nephew. When Whitefield preached in the Canongate parish church Ralph accompanied him to the pulpit ; 'whereat,' Whitefield writes, 'the people were ready to shout for joy, though I believe it gave offence to his associates.' Two days later, however, all was changed. Whitefield attended a meeting of the Associate Presbytery at Dunfermline, held for the express purpose of setting him right about Church government; but he proved an intractable pupil, saying that he had no scruples about Church government, and had given little attention to the questions which they raised. He went so far as to say that no one form of Church government had exclusive authority. Pointing to his heart, he said in his dramatic manner, 'I do not find it here.' This was too much for Moncrieff, who, the narrator says, being of a warm temper, gave a rap on the Bible which was lying on the table and replied, 'But I find it, *here.*' The Seceders' accounts of the discussion tally with Whitefield's, except in regard to the names of the different speakers, a detail upon which their authority must be preferred. He writes :—

'Dear Mr Erskine desired they would have patience with me, for that, having been born and bred in England, I could not be supposed to be perfectly acquainted with the nature of their Covenants. One, much warmer than the rest, immediately replied that no indulgence was to be shown me, that England had revolted most with respect to Church government, and that I, born and educated there, could not but be acquainted with the matter now in debate. . . . I asked them seriously, what they would have me to do. The answer was that I was not desired to immediately subscribe the Covenant, but to preach only for them, till I had further light. I asked, "Why only for them ?" Mr Ralph said, "They were the Lord's people." I then asked whether there were no other Lord's people but themselves. . . . Soon after this, the company broke up, and one of these otherwise venerable men went into the meeting-house, and preached a sermon, wherein he so spent himself in talking against prelacy that, when he came to invite poor sinners to Jesus Christ, his breath was gone and he could scarce be heard. . . . I retired, I wept, I prayed ; and, after preaching in the fields, dined with them and then took a final leave.'

The language here imputed to Ralph has frequently

been quoted by controversialists, eager to exhibit the Erskines as intolerant sectarians. But the words were not Ralph's. On the following Sunday he condemned, at the Communion Table, an opinion *which he heard one lately express*, that 'none have Christ's image who have not just our image,' as implying a separation from all the churches of Christ. Indeed Whitefield himself wrote to one of Ebenezer's sons: 'If all the Seceders were like-minded with your honoured father and uncle, matters would not be carried on with so high a hand.' Further disproof has recently come to light, in a letter written by Ralph to Whitefield within ten days of the meeting :—

'I weary to be long out of your company. I see a falsehood published in the late prints, that my brethren found fault with me for attending you to the Canongate Church; whereas not one of them ever opened his mouth to blame me. When I parted last with you, and reflected upon your declining conversation with my brethren on the subject of Church Government, you was represented to my mind as a young worker in the garden of God, occupied as yet only about the flowers, and unwilling to take any care of the hedges by which the garden should be fenced. Your refusing a close communing on this head seemed to me so far unlike the disposition which our former correspondence made me think you was of, that I was willing to ascribe it rather to the hurry of temptation for the time, amidst the ringing of bells for sermon, and some rash words uttered in your hearing, than to any contrary bias that now you have got.'

The letter, which is exceedingly long, goes on to express anxiety lest, in parish manses, Whitefield may gain a wrong impression of the Secession, and so be 'lost to us.' Yet he congratulates him on the welcome he is receiving, and on the liberality shown towards his Orphan scheme :—

'It could not have been so great among most of our adherents, who are generally of the poorer sort, and are not only much at under by the late dearth, but also by contributing their outmost for building kirks and raising stipends, for deposed and persecuted ministers.

Meantime you are now conversant with some of the ministry that dwell in their ceiled houses, and who, however good and sound some be, are, at best, suffering the house of the Lord to lye waste, and strengthening the hand of Church robbers, by their sinful mixtures with them in Church judicatories. . . . These are the greatest bars and impediments at present in the way of witnessing work, because their reputation as good men and sound preachers, and yet making no appearance, brings the work under disparagement. Glad shall I be if you come forth from all companies without a wrong impression of matters ; but if you shall be tinctured so far as to have light thoughts of the Assembly's sin, not only in deposing us, but in rejecting our testimony, and light thoughts of those that are at ease in Zion, and if you find yourself so entangled and chained, as not to be at liberty to give the certain sound in testimony in public against these as against other matters, I would fear that, whatever gain you obtain one way, you should go off with greater loss another, and with less inward peace . . . I would be loath to think of your going away under a suspicion among us, or of your being unwilling to know what government Christ has appointed in His word, as if it were a matter of moonshine, and unwilling to try whether the oath of God that Britain is under be a lawful oath or not . . . If you come to this side, I can by no means allow you to change your quarters. My wife and children salute you kindly and long to see you again. I doubt not but your Orphans will be remembered here by some that are not exhausted with other things.—Yours, as formerly, in our dear Lord Jesus, RALPH ERSKINE.'

Whitefield continued to frequent the 'ceiled houses,' and to regard Church government as 'moonshine.' In a few months, the rupture with the Seceders was complete, and they specifically condemned his work. In the first instance, it was his Episcopacy that provoked them, and in this they were at one with many Established Churchmen ; but their provocation became bitter, when the churches of men like Currie of Kinglassie were thronged by the crowds which he attracted. They denounced him as a friend of backsliders, and even as an enemy of the gospel. When, on his second visit to Scotland in 1742, he was invited to take part in the Cambuslang Revival, the Associate Presbytery appointed a day of fasting and humiliation for 'the countenance given to a priest of the Church of England, and for the symptoms of delusion attending the present awful work upon the bodies and spirits of men going on at Cambuslang.' Although the Erskines had no personal share in this enactment, their writings and sermons [1] were full of keen and unsparing criticism of the whole movement. Ebenezer wrote about those 'night-disciples, who had held back their testimony in a day of danger, and had now embraced a religion lying in internal feelings and introspection, and had yielded to the noisy wind, that the known foreigner of the prelatic communion had brought along with him into the land.' He pronounced it to be 'a hurtful and noxious wind,' and declared that one of its chief mischiefs lay in the popularity it brought to the corrupt judicatories. Ralph was as emphatic. Two of his ablest, if not best, publications, *Faith no Fancy* and *Fraud and Falsehood Discovered*, were given to this controversy, the burden of his argument being, that the Revival rested upon false doctrines and had dangerous tendencies.

The condemnation of the 'Cam'slang Wark' by the Seceders cannot fairly be ascribed to mere jealousy. Its wild and demonstrative excitement was at variance with their type of teaching. Two years before the difference with Whitefield arose, Ralph Erskine, in reply to a friendly inquiry from John Wesley, wrote that in Scotland conversion had not been accompanied by 'sudden and visible effects,' and that such effects should be discouraged.

'All the outward appearances of people's being affected among us in time of preaching, especially upon Sacramental occasions, may be re-

---

[1] The Erskines have been falsely credited with the authorship of an Act handing over Whitefield to Satan. That Act was passed in 1748 by the Antiburgher Synod, which handed them, too, to Satan.

duced to these two sorts. One is, hearing with a close silent attention, with gravity and greediness, discovered by fixed looks, weeping eyes, joyful or sorrowful-like countenances, evidencing tenderness in hearing. Another sort is, when the word is so affecting to the congregation as to make them lift up their voice and weep aloud, some more depressedly, others more highly, and at times the whole multitude in a flood of tears, all, as it were, crying out at once, till their voice be ready to drown out the minister's, so as he can hardly be heard for the weeping noise that surrounds him. . . . We judge that the more solid and judicious part of the auditory are seldom so noisy, though perhaps more affected inwardly. . . . A delusive spirit may sometimes lead poor souls to rest upon impressions, motions, and what they feel within them, as if these were to be the ground and reason of their hope. The true spirit of God within a believer leads him to a dependence upon Christ *without* him, and not upon a Christ *within* him, nor upon any created or communicated graces, gifts, experiences, tears, sorrows, joys, frowns, feelings, or whatever else. . . . He must be brought off from confidence in, or dependence upon, frames, enlargements, influences and attainments, to a solid life of faith, upon the grounds that are unchangeable.'

It is doubtful if men who took such a view could, in any circumstances, have concurred in a movement which filled churches and fields with panic-stricken crowds, expressing their contrition in convulsions and howls, and proving that they had been saved by lively narratives of their visions of the sufferings of the lost. The Erskines gained their hold upon Scotland by sober, meditative, and sacramental presentation of the gospel, with careful instruction in the Bible. If they had accepted the Cambuslang methods, the tone of their own revivalism would have been altered, and the Church they founded would have lost the features to which it owed its gradual but steady growth. In such a matter the judgment of history may be accepted. Religious emotionalism has found no permanent home in the Scottish lowlands.

Yet the controversy showed the Erskines personally at their worst. No doubt they had provocation. Some of the Established ministers, with a sneer which raises suspicion as to their motives in supporting Whitefield, taunted them with the fact that they no longer had a monopoly of conversions and of crowded churches. But they were unbridled in their resentment, and ignored the genuine and pious enthusiasm of men like M'Laurin and Robe. They wrote with a violence for which their apologists need to plead that it was usual in those days. For two or three years, the composure and calmness, which had carried them with dignity through the crisis of Secession, disappeared, and their extravagant severities encouraged among their followers a hard and violent spirit, for which, as next chapter will show, they had to pay a heavy penalty. It is pleasant to think that they paid it humbly, and with reconciliation. Whitefield's Journal for 1751 contains the following entry: ' I have met and shaken hands with Mr Ralph Erskine. Oh when will God's people learn war no more ! ' Whitefield went further. In a sermon preached after Ralph's death, he cited him as an example of ' God's triumphant saints.'

CHAPTER VIII

THE BREACH

THE events with which this chapter deals have usually been dismissed by the critics of the Erskines with a few words of reproach, and by their admirers with a few words of apology; yet, for a true understanding of their lives, there must be some definite acquaintance with facts which turned many of their friends and followers into bitter foes, and altered the course of their work.

It has been shown in the preceding chapter that two views, which were not logically consistent, appeared in the Secession documents, with regard to the relation between Church and State. The one fixed attention upon the recent backslidings of the Church, as the justification of Secession; the other, which was at once more conservative and more radical, looked upon the Revolution Settlement as inadequate at its best, and caught glimpses of a new ideal—the complete detachment of the Church from civil authority and influence. For a time, and until the Seceders were actually deposed, the two views co-existed without strife or even strain, but thereafter the divergence appeared. It first came to light with regard to the observance of a Fast appointed by Government. In 1741 the Associate Presbytery declared that it was unlawful for Seceders to observe any Fast so appointed, on the ground that the slightest recognition of the control of the State over the Church was an impingement upon the sole Headship of Christ. Against this decision the Erskines protested. In that

year Wilson, who had done more than any other to
indicate and vindicate a via media, died, and he was
succeeded in his Professorship by Moncrieff, who was
incapable of compromise. Moncrieff had among his
students a recruit from the Divinity Hall of the Established Church, Adam Gib, an acute, eager, and unsparing man, whose *View of the Covenant of Grace* secured
for him, apart from ecclesiastical affairs, a prominent
place among Scottish theologians. Moncrieff and Gib
became the nucleus of a group of men, who determined
to be more thorough than the Seceders had hitherto
been. They had less perspective, less balance, and they
were disqualified for wise leadership by a strong disposition to insist upon minute details; but they had
logic, so far, on their side, and they shrank back from
no opinion through fear of consequences. Their watchword was 'Progress in Covenanting Work,' and their
argument was that, in order to secure true independence
for the Church, there must be a complete revision of her
relations to the civil powers—that the ideal of the Reformation could be reached only by a forward movement.

They found a standing-ground, when the Associate
Presbytery made the renewal of the Covenants a term
of Church Communion. In 1744 Moncrieff represented
to the Presbytery that he had 'scruples.' As a consistent Covenanter he could not take the Burgess
Oath. 'He apprehended that, if the Presbytery examined the Oath, it would be found to be sinful.' The
Burgess Oath had originated in 1591,[1] at a time when
the Church claimed authority over the State. It varied

[1] The antiquity of the Oath was a leading point in the controversy.
Ralph Erskine traced it back to 1572, and Principal Lee proves that,
in Edinburgh at least, it was in force in 1591. In *The Social Life
of Scotland*, the controversy, which began in 1744, is ascribed to
"a new Oath imposed on all citizens in 1746." M'Kelvie gives the
date of the Edinburgh, Glasgow and Perth Oath as 1745!

in the seven or eight burghs in which it was enforced, but the forms prescribed in Edinburgh, Glasgow and Perth were first brought under discussion. The old Edinburgh form, which was reckoned the most offensive, ran as follows :—

'Heir I protest befoir God and your Lordship, that I profess and allow with my hairt, the trew religioun qlk at this present is publictlie preachit within this realme, and authorizit be the lawes thairof : I sall abyde therat and defend the samyn to my lyfis end, renouncing the Roman religioun callit papistrie.'

Moncrieff argued that the Secession rested upon the fact, that the true religion was not publicly preached and authorised in Scotland, and that therefore no consistent Seceder could take the Oath. That it had been taken for a century and a half without scruples, was nothing to him ; he had scruples, and with these the Presbytery must deal. It at once became apparent that he had many supporters. Several sessions transmitted overtures, which the newly formed Synod debated at great length, holding one special meeting after another. In April 1746, it was decided that 'no Seceder could, with safety of con-science and without sin, take the Burgess Oath, and that those who had already taken it should not be allowed to take the Covenant, until they compeared before their respective sessions and acknowledged a sense of their mistake.' From this meeting of Synod Ebenezer Erskine was absent, and at the next meeting in September he entered his dissent. Six months later, he proposed that the Synod, without reversing its decision, should remit the matter to presbyteries and sessions. Moncrieff and his friends opposed this, contending that the Secession Church was not bound by the Barrier Act ; and that, indeed, laymen were incompetent to deal with such a question. When they were outvoted, they withdrew from the Synod, and declared that they represented the true Church of Secession. In April 1747, they constituted themselves as a Church Court, the 'General Associate Synod,' and proceeded to deal with the majority according to Church forms. They libelled them, suspended them, and finally excommunicated them, handing them over to Satan, and declaring that they should be 'holden by the faithful as heathen men and publicans.' Ralph Erskine was excommunicated in 1749, and Ebenezer in 1750. Strange to say, half of the rapidly increasing congregations approved of the sentence, and sided with the General Associates, who were thenceforward known as Antiburghers, the Erskines and their adherents being styled Burghers. The division, which made its way into every hamlet where the Secession had established itself and created an absolute cleavage, was entitled 'The Breach.'

The contention had ludicrous aspects. It was waged with the utmost prolixity. In 1746, for instance, the Synod held, within six months, three special meetings, at each of which the question was discussed for a fortnight. Many of the points raised were verbal, unreal, or grotesque. Personalities abounded. The debates were always keen, and sometimes furious. The opponents of the Secession were furnished with many an occasion for derisive scorn, while some ministers in the Established Church, who had no disposition to deride, and who still cherished kindly feelings towards the Seceders, were confirmed in their reluctantly formed opinion that the Secession had been an unwise movement. The Erskines seemed to have let loose ideas and sentiments, of which they had not measured the inevitable developments and consequences. Their own contributions to the controversy were far below the level of their earlier speeches and writings. It lay with the devout and genial Ralph to present the issue to the Church in a literary shape,[1] and if the polemics he produced are

[1] Ralph's publications on the subject were numerous; the most important were *Fancy no Faith* and *Fancy still no Faith*.

marked by some devoutness, the devoutness is pugnacious, while his geniality is quite invisible.

Yet only a superficial judgment will pronounce the matter to have been trivial, or will condemn the Erskines for the position which they took and held. In all religious controversies, leaders are outrun by followers who push principles to extremes, and the leaders show real strength by refusing to advance beyond the limits of their own convictions. The opinion and intention of the Erskines would not allow them to deny that the true religion was publicly professed in Scotland, and recognised by law. Grave as had been the Assembly's errors, they were not prepared for a position of antagonism to the Revolution Settlement, which secured at least that the State remained religious, Christian, and Protestant by profession, and guaranteed the Presbyterianism of Scotland. A sentence from one of Ebenezer's speeches suffices to show that he steadily adhered to the position taken in 1733 :—

'We have made a Secession from the judicatories of the Established Church ; yet we never made a secession from the visible Church of Christ in Scotland—by no manner of means.'

Besides, Moncrieff's and Gib's contention seemed likely to lead to an abandonment of civic and political duty, on the ground of the religious defection of the nation, and to the creation of a church which would minimise or even deny the obligation of its members to the State. Such an attitude could not be accepted by the Erskines, in whom patriotism was engrained. It was impossible for them to admit that the 'sins of church judicatories' gave sufficient reason for declining to act as burgesses, or even that the failure of the State to discharge properly its religious functions cancelled its claims to their service in any department of civic life. It may be argued, and it was argued, that their position cannot be logically vindicated, and that as a matter of fact the State did not in their day 'main-

I

tain the true religion'; but it is a fair reply, that they showed both wisdom and courage in refusing to be driven from a position, which left room for hopes of the reformation of the State Church, on the basis of the Revolution Settlement, and for all the activities of Christian patriotism. It must also be recognised that they made no attempt to force any theory upon the Secession Church. They were anxious for toleration, and willing to accept a compromise. At one Synod they pled for delay. At another they offered to agree to anything, except the rigid rule that a faithful Seceder could not be a Burgess, and the bald declaration that the true religion was not recognised by the laws of Scotland.

The Antiburghers cannot indeed be commended, either for their logic or for their liberalism. If their logic had been thorough, it would have detached them wholly from public life, and led them straight into the camp of the Cameronians. But thither they had no mind to go.[1] They persisted in that devotion to the House of Hanover of which Gib had given proof in 1745. Their views on the Oath had little practical effect, for the number of burghs affected was limited, and, even in them, magistrates sometimes allowed burgesses, when signing, to append a protest against the Religious Clause. With this single and limited exception, they were as loyal and as patriotic as the Burghers, and, when the centenary of the Revolution Settlement came round, they agreed that, in spite of its 'lamentable defects,' it should be commemorated as a source of 'great and invaluable blessings.' Nor must it be supposed that their contention was in any sense a liberal one. They

[1] For ten years they made a crusade against other Oaths, dealing in turn with the Constable's Oath, the Churchwarden's Oath, the Chapman's Oath, and finally the Mason's Oath. This last baffled them, as they failed to ascertain the particulars, and they turned their attention, more profitably, to the scrutiny of Arminian errors.

objected to the Oath, not as a religious test, but as an inadequate religious test. They wished to increase and in-
tensify not to mitigate or remove it—to go backwards not
forwards. Their merit lay in this, that in seeking to go
backwards they were led to go forwards. Within twelve
years of the Breach, Moncrieff, who, with all his irascibility,
was conspicuously single-hearted and devoutly bold, proposed that they should petition the King to ' restore the
true religion'; but he was left pathetically alone, no
one seconding his proposal. The Antiburgher trend of
thought had taken the opposite direction, and inclined
to question seriously the religious functions of the State,
and the advantage of religious tests. Yet this change
was gradual, and it was checked by the doughty Gib—
Pope Gib he was called—who ruled the Antiburghers
as rigidly as Robertson ruled the Assembly. Among
the Burghers there was almost as much development.
In the main, however, both branches of the Seceders
were guided by the ideas of the Erskines, and, when
they united in 1820, it was through an agreement that
opinions upon such subjects should be ' matter of for-
bearance.' [1] The Erskines undoubtedly prevailed.

Yet into their own lives the Breach brought bitterness
and pain. For a time the Secession seemed to be mortally
wounded. Its position in the country was lowered. There
was some contraction in horizon, with depression if not
deterioration of religious tone. The personalities which
entered into the discussion deprived the Church of the
dignity which it had hitherto maintained, as a movement
which was national in its motives and ideals, and greatly
lessened the force of its appeal to the Christian intelligence of Scotland. Church historians who have thought
it proper to draw a veil over the events above described,

[1] The Burgess Oath was abolished in 1819; but the abolition of it
was not the cause of the Union, which had been under discussion for
ten or eleven years.

have concealed the chief hindrance which the Secession encountered in its infancy. The hindrance was a very powerful one, limiting its attractiveness and narrowing its compass. Of this the Erskines were aware, and therefore they deplored the Breach, as an irreparable injury to the work of their lives.

In the case of both brothers there was the added bitterness of family dissension. Ebenezer's favourite daughter, 'Ailie,' was married to a Secession minister, James Scott of Gateshaw, who sided with the Antiburghers. With true chivalry Ebenezer refrained from increasing his daughter's perplexity, but she decided between her father and her husband with admirable precision. When her husband returned from the Synod which excommunicated the Erskines, she met him at the manse-door with an anxious look. He came with bent head and in evident distress. 'Well?' she said. He was silent. She followed him into his study and repeated her query—'Well?' After a long pause he replied, 'We have excommunicated them.' 'You have excommunicated my father and my uncle ! You are my husband, but never more shall you be minister of mine.' She kept her word, and joined the Burgher congregation at Jedburgh. It is to her husband's credit that he showed no resentment, and every Sunday morning mounted her on his pony, that she might ride to Jedburgh to profit by ministrations which preserved the loved traditions of the Portmoak Manse.

Ralph, who had been far keener in the controversy, had a much heavier penalty to pay. Of three sons who were Secession ministers, two sided with him ; but the third, John, minister of Leslie, became, after some hesitation, an Antiburgher. If Mrs Scott represented Scotland's religious women at their best, John Erskine represented religious Scotsmen at their worst. When Ralph entered the Dunfermline Presbytery, at the meeting immediately after the Breach, the Presbytery, by a majority, refused him leave to speak, and declared him not a member of the court. Writing to another son, he says: 'He (John) sat there, with the Presbytery which exauctorated you and me and all the true, lawful Synod. You may be sure it was as a sword piercing my heart, to see Johnny sitting in the midst of them.' Yet he forgave Johnny, invited him to the manse, and when evening came, asked him to conduct worship. The hard youth —he was only twenty-seven—thought it right to pray that 'the Lord would restore his father to his former usefulness.' He went still further. It was reported to the Antiburghers that one of their number, Patrick Matthew of Midlem, in whose manse Ralph happened to be a guest, had asked him to conduct worship. The Presbytery dealt with Matthew, for this disregard of the Synod's excommunication. The culprit admitted under pressure that he had 'thoughtlessly given offence,' but declined to acknowledge that he had 'committed a sin.' He was brought before the Supreme Court, which censured and suspended him. Ultimately it was resolved to depose him, and, with a harshness which was almost savage, John Erskine was appointed to conduct the devotions of the Synod which carried out the deposition. He fulfilled the appointment without a word of filial protest. A worse tale went abroad— that when he was dying, a few months later, he refused reconciliation with his loving father; but the tale lacks evidence, and must be discredited. That it was circulated even among enemies, shows what Ralph had to bear.

Nothing is finer in the Erskines' lives than the spirit in which they faced those trials. As in the case of the noblest sufferers in the preceding century, experiences which would have hardened and embittered ordinary men gave them a new tenderness and tolerance. Ebenezer

wrote to a friendly Established Church minister, who had
expressed sympathy :—

'Here is comfort, in case of rents, divisions, and manifold disorders
in the visible Church, as there are at this day. The great Master of
the House is looking on. He permits and over-rules all these disorders
for His own holy and wise ends, for the trial of faith and patience,
and to show His own skill in bringing order out of confusion.'

As Ralph's wounds were deeper, so were his con-
solations. The tidings of his deposition, to which his
son had assented, reached him when he was celebrating
Communion in the open air, within sight of the Portmoak hills, where in student days he had heard God's
voice. One of the communicants writes :—

'When the news was brought, he began to falter in speech, but
lifting up his eyes towards Portmoak, he said : "My soul is cast
down within me : therefore will I remember Thee, from the land of
Jordan and of the Hermonites, and from the hill Mizar." His
troubled soul was calmed, and he went through his work with his
usual animation. . . . "After you have drunk a cup of trembling,"
he said, "expect a cup of comfort."'

Still more striking is it, that, when it fell to him to
preach, at the opening of the first Burgher Synod, he had
courage to tell his associates that they partly owed their
calamity to their past severity towards the Established
Church. He carefully examined the causes of God's
judgment, and placed among them :—

'Untenderness towards those we left in the judicatories, when we
made secession from them, without dealing more kindly with them,
praying more for them, and bearing more with them, especially
such as were friends to the same Reformation cause, though not
enlightened in the same manner of witnessing for it. Though we
began with some moderation towards them, yet many proceeded
soon to such heights as could not in the issue but terminate in a
downfall. . . . If the bond of brotherly love was too soon broken,
the Lord is righteous in ordering such a breach as threatens to

destroy the temple, and to make us read our sin in our punishment. Though we were not equally chargeable in this way, yet we have been too indulgent to those that were so, and therefore cannot purge ourselves.'

While the Breach brought to light the mischiefs of a schismatic temper, it showed that the Erskines had nothing of the spirit which prides itself on schism, and it established their title to be regarded as men of deep and humble religion.

CHAPTER IX

AFTER THE BREACH

AT the date of the Breach, the Erskines were past mid-life, Ebenezer being 67 and Ralph 62; but they had still work to do, and strength to do it. Their remaining years were given to their parochial duties, and to the guidance of the life of the Secession Church. They had no further public controversy, and their personal devoutness asserted itself with much attractive power, both in their own parishes and in the Burgher Synod, where their influence was now undisputed.

The first concern of the Synod was to prevent the recurrence of division, by defining more clearly their relation to the Church of Scotland. With this in view, they revised the Testimony of 1736, not altering it in essentials, but supplementing it at points, and emphasising their special view of the matters which had caused dissension. This Revised Testimony, which was prepared by Ebenezer, was formally adopted as a symbol, though not a standard, of the Burgher Church.

At the same time the Erskines and Fisher were entrusted with a scheme which had more important results— the drafting of an ' Explication of the Assembly's Shorter Catechism.' The intention was to popularise the teaching of the Confession, and specially to show its consistency with the doctrines of free grace. The scheme was carried out with great care and success. The Catechism, popularly known as ' Fisher's Catechism,' bore neither touch nor tinge of recent controversies, and was in no sense sectarian. So competent a theologian as Dr John Brown has said that 'it contains, within the shortest compass, the fullest and the clearest exposition of Christian doctrine and law that is to be found in any language.' If this is a somewhat partial estimate, the Catechism is certainly a remarkable production, showing a rare balance of thought and lucidity of language. For several generations it held an important place in Scottish religious life. While it restrained the evangelical zeal of the Seceders from antinomian excesses, it was widely read and accepted as a manual within the Established Church, and so contributed to maintain unity of Christian thought and feeling.[1]

The same concern for the doctrinal and devotional life of the Secession was shown in various measures for the development of fellowship and prayer throughout the Church; but its most interesting phase appears in a curious attempt to utilise Ralph Erskine's poetical gifts. The Synod of 1748 recommended him 'to have under his consideration a translation of the Songs of Scripture into metre, except the Psalms of David which are already translated, agreeable to the recommendation of the General Assembly of 1647.' A committee which was appointed to assist Ralph was discreet enough to leave the work entirely in his hands; but, even with this freedom, he was hampered by the obligation to use the so-called Common Metre, and by a laborious desire for literal adherence to the text. It cannot be said that the 'Scripture Songs,' which resulted, are among the happiest of his productions; yet some of the best couplets were appropriated by the editors of

[1] The Catechism was issued in two parts, in 1753 and 1761. Questions 8-25 were written by Ebenezer, Questions 76-95 by Ralph; but their influence pervades the whole Catechism. The title, 'Fisher's Catechism,' is due to its having been finally edited by Fisher after the death of the Erskines.

the 'Scottish Paraphrases,' and thus gained a place in the worship of all Presbyterian churches.[1]

It will be noted that this movement was expressly based upon a decision of the General Assembly. This is only one example of a steady desire to preserve identity with the Church of Scotland, which showed itself in many other ways. At the Visitation of Presbyteries, for example, one of the questions asked by Synodical authority was: 'Hath your Presbytery a Bible, a Confession of Faith, and a copy of the Acts of Assembly, before them at their several meetings?' Candidates for the ministry attended the lectures of Established Church professors. Although Ebenezer was appointed Professor of the Secession, he met with the students only for a few weeks yearly; and the devotional tone of his first students, among whom were John Brown of Haddington and M'Ewen, author of *The Types*, gives an accurate idea of the note which the Erskines sounded after the Breach. The practice of Covenanting was quietly dropped. No further objections were raised to the Oaths of Assurance and Allegiance, and friendly relations were resumed with evangelical ministers in the Established Church. When Willison of Dundee was dying in 1750, Ralph, who had often crossed swords with him, was beside him as a comforter. A foolish lady tried to revive the quarrel by saying to Ralph that there would be no Secession in heaven; but the two men smiled, and Willison nodded assent to Ralph's retort: 'Madam, in heaven there will be a complete Secession—from sin and sorrow.'

Yet there was no trace of wavering or of regret for the

---

[1] When seventy years ago a larger share in the authorship of the *Paraphrases* was claimed for Ralph, the claim was keenly disputed. The above statement rests upon an examination of the dates. The *Paraphrases*, as now in use, were first sanctioned by the Assembly in 1781.

Secession. Their sermons were full of appeals to their hearers to set the Gospel and the liberty of the Church above all else, and to reckon the advantages of Establishment as trifles in comparison. They contended against the growing latitudinarianism of the Established Church with all their former freedom and vigour. The only difference was, that, in their parochial work and their evangelistic tours, they were more studiously concerned than before with the development of the doctrinal and spiritual life of the Church.

At this stage there was ample vindication of the Seceders in the course of events within the General Assembly. Patrons who were legally disqualified devised a way of evading the law. They transferred their duties to qualified persons, usually their own factors, giving them at the same time the names of the persons to be presented; and the protests raised in the Assembly against this evasion were feeble and ineffective. Patronage itself had now gained open and able advocates, who resolved to have done with compromise, and to compel Presbyteries to enforce the law of the land. In 1751 a crisis was reached, in the Assembly's treatment of the Presbytery of Linlithgow, which had declined to induct a presentee against the will of parishioners. In presenting the case, the Presbytery urged that the Assembly was pursuing a ruinous policy, by 'compelling men to act in contradiction to the sense and persuasion of their own minds,' that loyal churchmen were being driven into Secession, and that the first principles of Presbyterianism were being abandoned. The Assembly, however, gave no heed to the plea, and pronounced a censure on the Presbytery. Indeed there was a party which maintained that a mere censure was insufficient, and proposed that the Presbytery should be suspended. This party was led by John Home, the author of *Douglas*, and William Robertson of Gladsmuir, who, though they were defeated in this contention, became thenceforward the rulers of the Assembly, partly through their remarkable ability, and partly through the consistency of their policy. They frankly set aside the idea of 'a call,' and insisted that a presentation should in all cases be carried out, 'without any reservation founded on the merits of the call, or any reckoning of the number of heritors, elders, or parishioners, who concurred or dissented.' When parishioners proved refractory, they did not hesitate to call in the help of soldiers. In one parish after another, presentees were taken to their manses under military guard, and not without riot. This policy developed with a rapidity which historians have found it difficult to explain. In 1752 the Assembly, by ninety-three to sixty-five votes, deposed Thomas Gillespie of Carnock, a blameless and devout minister, because he refused to take part in an enforced settlement. Another schism was thus created; for Gillespie, continuing his ministry, became the founder of the Relief Church, which for nearly a century contended separately, yet with views which gradually approached those of the Seceders, for the rights of conscience and the purity of the Gospel.[1] Robertson and Home however persisted, and indeed showed some satisfaction in ridding the Church of men whose doctrines were as distasteful as their Church principles.

Meanwhile Moderatism took shape and grew apace. England as well as Scotland was astonished by the growth. In 1751 John Wesley made the first of his twenty-two visits to Scotland, being 'specially urged by the abounding Arianism and Socinianism of the country.' He received a more friendly welcome than he expected, but subsequently he was shocked by the secular demeanour of the members of Assembly, who left all church affairs in the hands of a troop of lawyers. Although he was cordially admitted by many parish ministers to their

[1] In 1847, the Relief and Secession Churches united, and became the 'United Presbyterian Church.'

pulpits, and preached there to crowded congregations, he made no impression upon the policy of the Church. The difference between Wesley and the Erskines, as to methods and some doctrines, in no way alters the fact, that the same causes, which attracted crowds of Established Church people to Wesley's preaching, steadily swelled the ranks of the Secession Church. The Church of Scotland was now fairly under a regime which certainly, however one may estimate its literary and intellectual effect, ruled evangelical earnestness out of parish churches, or tolerated it contemptuously.

The increase of Secession was in one respect fostered rather than hindered by the Breach. Scotland was at that time under-churched, and the Moderate party, for its own reasons, was strongly opposed to church-extension. The erection of new places of worship met a real necessity, and every meeting-house, whether Burgher or Antiburgher, became a new centre of religious life. Those who were dissatisfied with the preaching of the Moderates could now choose between the two types of dissent, furnished by the two branches of the Secession. Within seven years of the Breach, the Secession congregations numbered 105, and almost every annual meeting of the Assembly gave some new offence, which laid the foundation of five or six additional congregations.

The Erskines viewed this progress without exultation. They deplored the cause of it, and their sense of responsibility for the guidance of the Church increased with their years. Far from showing any eagerness in organisation, they refrained from initiating church-extension schemes of any sort. With a resolute conservatism, they insisted that all the operations of the Church should be in accordance with church law. There was a dearth of candidates for the Burgher ministry, most of the Secession students having been attracted in their youthful keenness by the Antiburgher theory, but it never occurred to them that the emergency might be met by ordaining untrained men. The preaching of laymen was in their eyes a gross offence against Church order. Thus, year after year, they were obliged to refuse scores of requests for 'sermon' from distressed parishes, and with every year their physical ability for evangelistic journeyings was reduced. Ralph's correspondence shows that, in one fortnight, he preached twenty sermons, to which the people listened 'as if they were getting their first offer of Christ and of salvation, and as if the Word were going through heart and flesh.' The strain such labour caused could not long be borne. Yet they kept their cheerfulness, and did not allow themselves to be fretted. Ebenezer was a frequent and a welcome visitor at the Stirling bowling-green, and Ralph's verses flowed with a new softness, in lines such as these :—

> 'Happy the company that's gone
> From cross to crown, from thrall to throne ;
> How loud they sing upon the shore
> To which they sailed in heart before !

> 'Death from all death hath set us free
> And will our gain for ever be ;
> Death loosed the massy chain of woe,
> To let the mournful captives go.

> 'Death is to us a sweet repose,
> The bud is ope'd to show the rose ;
> The net is broke to let us fly
> And build our happy nest on high.'

Ralph, although the younger, was first to bend beneath the weight of years. In 1751 he and his congregation were anxious that his son James should be ordained as his colleague, and the young man shared the desire. It was a serious blow when the Synod intervened, and appointed James colleague to his uncle Ebenezer at Stirling. The father's unfitness for pastoral duties was hastened by the development of heart disease, for which the medical science of Dunfermline had no remedy but 'copious bleeding.' Arrangements made in April, 1751, for the disposal of his modest property, show that he had death in view, yet he persevered in his ministry, devoting his spare hours to the completion of the Scripture Songs. His last public duty was discharged on October 23, 1752, when he drafted a petition to the King, on behalf of 'the peace and quiet of His Majesty's most loyal subjects in Ireland.' On the following Sunday, after preaching to his congregation on the text, 'All her paths are peace,' he was seized by a nervous fever, which rapidly became fatal. Two other members of the household were laid low at the same time, and his loving nature was perturbed by the absence of friendly faces from his sick-room; but before the end came, he gained composure. His last words were: 'I shall be for ever a debtor to free grace. Victory, victory, victory!' He died on November 6, 1752, in the sixty-eighth year of his age.

Ebenezer had a longer and severer struggle with weakness. When he entered his seventieth year he resigned his professorship. One of his pupils described his last lecture in simple but graphic words :—

'He dismissed the students, being no more to teach them, with a solemn prayer, and dedication of them to the work of the ministry, in a manner the like whereof I was never witness unto; no, nor ever will.'

Thenceforward he limited himself to preaching and to pastoral work, with occasional appearances at public gatherings. The death of his second wife, in 1751, struck a blow at his remaining strength, and gastric troubles, which had distressed him for many years, became more frequent and more serious. The appointment of James as his colleague revived his energy, and seemed for a time likely to prolong his working days. In the Ordination sermon which he preached on the occasion—'Gospel-treasure in Earthen Vessels'—a ring of defiance blends with a pathetic strain :—

'The ministers of Christ are but tender wear, and had need to be tenderly handled; for an earthen vessel is soon staved and broken into shells, and then is of no more use. Your ministers are men of like passions and infirmities, of body and mind, with yourselves, and stand much in need of your sympathy, especially considering that the strength of battle from hell and earth is against them. What dashing and harsh treatment some of these earthen vessels have met with in Stirling, is pretty well known. Some of them have been stoned; some have had their hoary hairs brought to the grave with sorrow; and another hath been cast out of the legal synagogue and maintenance, for bearing testimony against the sins of the place, and the tyranny and defection of the judicatories of the Church of Scotland. These things I mention, not out of resentment, but that I may be found a faithful witness for the Lord against the sins of the place. The Magistrates and Town-council of Stirling must answer unto God for what they have done in this matter. All that I shall say upon this head is, with my royal Master, when they were taking away His life, Father, forgive them, for they know not what they do; and with the proto-martyr Stephen, when they were stoning him to death, and when he was going out of Time into Eternity, Lord, lay not this sin to their charge.'

In the face of such words, it is preposterous to say, as controversialists have said, that he cherished the idea of returning to the Established Church. Yet even on such an occasion he refrained from enlarging upon the ecclesiastical position of the Seceders, and said not a word about the relation between Church and State. His main theme was the duty of Christian ministers to preach the gospel to the poor.

'Some prefer a gingle of words, a flourish of heathen morality, unto the gospel of Christ; they choose rather to have their ears tickled with the words of men's wisdom, than to have their hearts touched, and their souls fed and nourished, with the plain and simple truths of the everlasting gospel. They that are of this spirit plainly declare their palate is vitiate with some dreadful, foul distemper or other; their understandings are darkened, and their affections taken up with some other thing than precious Christ, and His unsearchable riches. And I may say of such ministers as entertain their hearers with those flourishes of rhetoric, and moral harangues, instead of preaching Christ and the supernatural mysteries of Christianity, whatever be their character among their votaries, they are ministers of Satan, transforming themselves into ministers of Christ, and that awful word is but too applicable to them and their abettors, "They are blind guides: and if the blind lead the blind, both shall fall into the ditch." '

His health revived for a few months, but in autumn the old ailments returned, and, when his brother died in November, he was a partial invalid. He is said to have received the tidings quietly, with the words: 'And is Ralph gone? He has twice got the start of me; he was first in Christ, and now he is first in glory.' On the following Sunday he struggled out of bed and preached a short and cheering sermon on the words, 'I know that my Redeemer liveth.'

It was his last appearance in the pulpit; but he had still to bear eighteen months of extreme weakness and pain, aggravated by the crude surgery of the times. In his sufferings he was tended by a loving daughter, and supported by the reverential and almost worshipping concern of his congregation, and of the whole Secession Church. The following letter, addressed to his daughter, Mrs Scott, bears the date '1753.'

'According to the course of nature, it was my turn to have gone off before your dear Uncle Ralph. But the will of the good and sovereign God has determined that I should tarry behind for a while, in this weary wilderness. It seems I am not yet made meet to be a partaker of the inheritance of the saints in light, but need to be more beaten with the hammer of affliction, before I come to the upper temple and sanctuary. Good is the will of the Lord. I am mostly confined to my bed. I sometimes get up, but in a little I am forced to return, through pain, which abates, as to the severity of it, whenever I get to bed; insomuch that my tottering hand becomes steady, and both body and mind are more easy. This letter is a proof, for it is wrote in bed—leaning on my elbow. The Lord makes me to sing of mercy

K

on this account, that my bed is made to ease me and my couch to comfort me ; nor am I, like poor Job, scared with dreams, or terrified with visions. Many a time my meditations of Him are sweet, in the silent watches of the night. Many, many a time the Lord says, I am the Lord thy God ; and then follows, Oh my soul, thou hast said unto the Lord, Thou art my God ; Thine am I, Oh David, and on Thy side will I be, Thou Son of Jesse.'

Throughout his illness, his general demeanour and his occasional sayings disclosed that deep, brave, quiet piety which has been distinctive of Scottish religion. 'I have always,' he said, 'found my times of severe affliction my best times. Many blasts I have endured through life ; but I had this comfort under them—a good God, a good conscience, a good cause.' When one of his elders asked him, 'Sir, you have given us many good advices ; may I ask what you are now doing with your own soul,' he replied, 'I am just doing with it what I did forty years ago ; I am resting on that word, "I am the Lord thy God."' Another friend, surprised at his serenity, asked him if he was not afraid of his sins. 'Indeed, no,' he answered ; 'ever since I knew Christ, I have never thought highly of my frames and duties, nor am I slavishly afraid of my sins.' One of his relatives thought to console him by expressing a hope, in the language of the school of Rutherford, that he would now and then get a *blink* to bear him up when in pain. He promptly replied, 'I know more of words than of blinks. "Though He slay me, yet will I trust in Him." The covenant is my charter. If it had not been for the blessed Word, my hope and strength had perished from the Lord. I have known more of God since I came to this bed than through all my life.'

So the months wore on, weakening him in body but not in spirit. The thoughts of both Secession Churches were turned towards Stirling. The Antiburghers forgot that they had handed him over to Satan. From Sunday to

Sunday, in rural meeting-houses, it was solemnly but thankfully recognised that the leader of the Secession was giving proof of the strength and purity of his religion. Now and then children were taken to his sickroom for baptism, and fragments of the brief sermons which, according to Church law, he preached before each baptism, propped up on pillows, were reported by the hearers and passed from lip to lip. This concluding chapter of his ministry made a permanent impression upon the Church, and went far to remove the acrimony which controversy had necessarily fostered.

In the spring of 1754 his pains became intense, but his courage stood the strain. 'Oh, sirs,' he said to his distressed friends, 'my body is indeed become a very disagreeable habitation for my soul; but when my soul forsakes the tabernacle of clay, it will fly as naturally to my Saviour's bosom as a bird to its loved nest.' In the early morning of the 1st of June, he awoke from a brief sleep, and asked his daughter, Mrs Fisher, who was at his bedside, what book she was reading. 'Your own sermon, father,' she replied, 'on the text "I am the Lord thy God."' 'Oh, woman,' he said, 'that is the best sermon ever I preached.' It was a sermon which had led to many conversions. A few minutes later, feeling the approach of darkness, he asked her to bring the candle quite close to him, and then laid his hand under his cheek, closed his eyes, and breathed out his soul.

He had all but completed the 74th year of his age and the 51st year of his ministry. In accordance with his request, his body was interred in his own church. The inscription, which is in Latin, states without any encomium that he fell asleep in Jesus after a very faithful ministry, and that he desired to be buried there, in order that, after death, he might confirm the testimony to which he had adhered throughout life. He was entitled to the desire. He had borne a testimony and he had adhered to it.

CHAPTER X

RESULTS

THE writings of the Erskines had a wide and definite influence which lasted for nearly a century.[1]

Ebenezer, though not reckoning himself an author, published many sermons, and in 1761 these were collected into four volumes by his son-in-law Fisher. Another volume, containing sermons not previously printed, was edited by one of his sons immediately after his death. It is impossible to enumerate the reprints, which appeared in Scotland, England, Ireland and America, between 1761 and 1830, when the demand for them abated. Some of the reprints consist of sermons bearing upon special topics, and others profess to be complete editions. The edition of 1761, however, is alone authentic. In later editions there are editorial alterations, some ordinary, some extraordinary. The removal of occasional Scotticisms, and the omission of sentences which seemed redundant, may be pardoned, though the Scotticisms removed are picturesque without vulgarity, and the style is so concise that abbreviation makes the meaning indistinct. It is different with alterations which affect the substance of the sermons, and these abound. In the absence of worthy evangelical literature, at the end of

[1] The only languages into which they are known to have been translated are Dutch and Welsh. It is said that in Holland they are still largely circulated as *Erskeyna.*

148

the eighteenth century and the beginning of the nineteenth, several editors took the liberty of circulating Ebenezer's clear and well-balanced presentation of Gospel truth, deleting sentences, and even paragraphs, which did not coincide with their own doctrinal views. The chief offenders were Wesleyan Methodists. In 1827, for instance, a series of the sermons was issued for the use of local preachers, ' carefully abridged, *corrected*, and revised,' the doctrines of Election and Perseverance being specially excluded. More kindly but scarcely less injurious treatment has been applied by admiring editors. In order to propitiate readers attached to the Established Church, they have omitted controversial passages, without which the train of argument is scarcely intelligible. Even a semi-official edition, issued in 1848, commits this error. The overkind editor not only inserts ' connecting words and phrases,' but ' adds from one discourse what seemed to him to be wanting in another, in order to make the doctrinal system complete.' The natural result of this two-fold process is that the Sermons are deprived of their original terseness and verve, and have a cumbrous lengthiness for which the author is not responsible.

Yet even with this ill-treatment, Ebenezer's sermons have probably had more influence than any of his brother's prose writings. Ralph's style was more finished, but it sometimes wandered into over-subtlety, and every now and then it broke into a vivid and almost fierce thrust, impressive at the time, but repellant to the later reader.[1] In his controversial writings, which give the best proof of his ability, he was minutely critical. No one outside

---

[1] An intelligent writer in the Scottish Biographical Dictionary (1833) says that Ralph's writings have ' stood a century of criticism, and are as much valued by pious and discerning readers as on the day when they were first published.' Some writings 'stand a century,' but no more.

Scotland, and few even in Scotland, could follow him with much interest into the details of his contention with the Antiburghers, and his writings against Whitefield have not much insight or outlook. Those of his published sermons which are exclusively devotional and expository lack the strength of thinking by which men's minds are guided. The highest place that can be given him among Scottish writers of his school is next to Thomas Boston. That, however, is a high place, and Boston wrote nothing like the Gospel Sonnets, the Believer's Jointure, or the Believer's Lodging. Within forty years of Ralph's death, no fewer than twenty-four editions of the Sonnets were published. In a former chapter it has been recognised that they have no enduring claim to recognition as poetry; but for a time their influence was as marked as their popularity. In dreary days, when religion was dull, dry and negative, they secured a welcome and a home for those doctrines of grace which were the supreme concern of both brothers. For modern readers the Sonnets have little attractiveness; but any competent critic will find in them freshness, strength, and piety, more than sufficient to explain their influence.

It was not, however, in their books that the Erskines left their best work, but in the religious history and the Church life of Scotland. Apart from personal and passing results, they created a channel for the gospel outside the Established Church. They did this deliberately, and the stream that flowed into the channel refreshed the thirsty land. Their Secession was prompted by a strong and irrepressible evangelicalism which could not rest satisfied with its own piety and orthodoxy in a time of darkness, and they wrote this on the banner of the Church they founded. Upon fidelity in preaching the gospel the Secession Church depended for its first growth, for the inward strength which carried it through futile controversies, for its continued vitality, for the healing of its breaches, and for the subsequent increase of its influence upon the social and religious life of Scotland.

It has frequently been argued that the Erskines would have better served the cause they had at heart if they had remained within the Established Church, and that indeed their Secession largely contributed to the triumph of Moderatism. No reader of the foregoing pages is likely to endorse this criticism. It was impossible for them, without cowardly inconsistency, to withdraw from the position into which conscience led them. There is puerility, and something worse, in discussing what would have happened if conscience had suffered them to temporise or compromise. It can never be right, for men who think that truth is in peril, to suppress their opinion, in the hope that afterwards they may have an opportunity of speaking. Further, it is an over-estimate of their powers to say that they could have checked the tide which swayed the Established Church. At the most they might have given a little more tenacity and visibility to the evangelical minority, and this would have been a doubtful benefit. In a popularly constituted Church, two elements so divergent could not have existed side by side without incessant strife. After twenty years' experience of varying contention, they judged it right to accept the position created for them by providence, and, as a separate body, to carry their message through Scotland, without the hindrances created by Church Courts which had an entirely different conception of the mission of the Church. History cannot refute such a judgment.

While they thought that separation was desirable in the interests of truth, the Moderates reached the same conclusion in the interests of peace. In 1765, an overture reached the Assembly, asking the Court to pay heed to the very remarkable progress of the 'schism in this Church.' A committee which was appointed to consider the subject reported, in 1766, in favour of the overture, stating that there were now 120 Secession churches, with 100,000 worshippers, that the Established Church was in danger, and that the Assembly should set itself to remedy the evils which caused secession. There was a keen debate, in the course of which Robertson maintained that schism was 'not an evil, but a beauty' in a Church, and other Moderates urged that schism, if mischievous, was inevitable. Robertson was too wise a man to be blind to all the merits of the Seceders. When a student, he had listened to their preaching on the East Lothian moors. 'Even yet,' he wrote in his maturity, 'the recollection thrills through my mind. The preacher addressed his audience in a strain of natural and profound eloquence. I was deeply affected, and I recollect more of that sermon than of any I have heard.' Yet he had no wish to bring back to the Assembly, of which he was ruler, men who were tenaciously opposed to his policy at every vital point ; and under his guidance, by ninety-nine votes to eighty-five, the proposal was set aside. This was the end of the matter, and the Seceders themselves were glad it went no further. Widely as they differed from Robertson, they were at one with him in thinking that their mission lay outside the Established Church.

The more quietly one thinks of the course of Scottish religion, the clearer does it become that Robertson and the Seceders were right. If Presbyterianism had continued to be the old, exclusive, domineering creed of the Covenants, it would either have crushed the spirit of the people, or the spirit of the people would have shaken it off. Among the Moderates, religion gained breadth, if not depth, assimilated foreign ideas, and held out a yielding hand to every kindly and discriminating stranger. It was better that this should be, without strife. In incessant strife, it would perhaps have been impossible. Yet if the Moderates had had all their own way, and had dragged the whole of Scotland at their heels, Scottish religion would have lost its identity, toned down to suit English ideas, and absorbed in easy, compliant sentiments. Something far broader than a sectarian interest was secured, by the creation of a Church, which was expressly Scottish, which claimed no share in the half-social, half-literary sympathies that looked across the Tweed with deference, and which was ashamed, rather than proud, of approximation to England. It is true that within the Established Church this patriotic sense was strong, all through the eighteenth century. It completely pervaded some classes of society, and over almost every class it had a certain influence. But in the Assembly it had a weak and faltering voice. The clearer expression given to it by the Seceders defined the convictions and feelings of many who did not belong to their number, and of some who condemned them for having left the Established Church. Even socially and intellectually, the Secession helped to maintain Scottish nationality, at a time when it was in danger of being absorbed. Spiritually, it had a far more definite worth. It detached the distinctive beliefs of the Reformed Church of Scotland from the fluctuating opinions of the Assembly, and preserved them through the very detachment. History never tells what might have been, but it furnishes parallels which, so far, guide in judgment; and, in this matter, a true historical parallel has been adduced by one of the wisest sons of the Secession Church.

'In Germany,' writes Dr John Ker, 'the corresponding movement of Spener and Francke died away under the advance of Rationalism, when, so far as we can see, the history of the Protestant Church in that country might have been a very different one if it had possessed a free evangelical church, which could have appealed to the people before they were dragged into indifferentism. The dread of breaking uniformity has been well nigh the ruin of life and unity. Another case is nearer home. Who can think that John Wesley and his friends would have done so much for the cause of Christ, in England and throughout the world, if they had been persuaded to take the step they were once inclined to, and had remained in the Anglican Church?

Long since, the ripples would have closed over their movement, instead of those currents that are finding their way to the end of the earth. Far from the secession of the Erskines retarding the return of evangelical life in Scotland, it was this, above all, which helped to preserve it in the National Church, and which stimulated its revival.'

To set on foot a Church expressly evangelical, was, however, only one side of the Erskines' work. They reached, declared, and formulated ideas of Christian liberty. For the first time they brought the doctrine of the Headship of Christ, which since the Reformation has been dear to Scotsmen, into connection with the modern claim for liberty of conscience. They saw with a growing clearness that the freedom of the Church can be vindicated, only on a theory which also vindicates the liberty of the individual, and that a truly free Church can never be tyrannical. Without contesting, or even disavowing, the ultramontane claims of seventeenth-century Presbyterianism, they took a position which made those claims meaningless, asserting, both by their example and by their teaching, that the Church must guard the freedom of her members, and that in religion freedom means equality. The fact that those ideas were not the outcome of mere theory increased the effectiveness with which they were presented. At the root of their action lay a double claim, (1) that a Christian must have liberty to speak his mind; (2) that all Christians are entitled to equal treatment in the Church. The importance of the claim lay in its being a religious claim, resting on the belief that the rights of the Church, and the rights of the humblest Church member, are alike derived from God.

To modern ears this has a familiar sound, but at the beginning of the eighteenth century it was a new thing in the land. The Erskines reached the belief by degrees, in the course of their contest with Church courts which disregarded the freedom of the Church and the freedom of her members. It could neither be defined nor acted upon, within the State Church. A new standing-ground was needed, and they saw the necessity. They made the Secession a home for ideas of Christian liberty and equality, and in that new home the ideas grew. The growth was slow, and it had curious and contradictory phases. The Erskines were nearly half a century in their graves before the Seceders formally declared that they could not accept the Confession of Faith without a public disavowal of 'compulsory and persecuting principles'; but, even then, they were half a century in advance of other Presbyterian Churches, and when once they reached that point Burghers and Antiburghers set aside their differences, and moved forward together to still more thorough ideas of freedom. While such thoughts gained ground among them, they possessed liberties which the Established Church did not, and could not give. They built churches, chose ministers, settled points of doctrine, administered Church discipline, and framed Church laws, at a time when other Scotsmen were hampered, in all these matters, by the authority of patrons and of parliaments. Claiming the privilege of Church government, they accepted, with it, the burden of Church support, and trained their adherents into the conviction that the Church could thrive and multiply without extraneous aid. In parish after parish, groups of farmers, shepherds and tradesmen discovered that, with some self-sacrifice, they could make their religion independent, not only of Assembly majorities, but of lairds and teinds. If the discovery sometimes led to self-assertion and pugnacity of temper, that was only the inevitable result of a new-born sense of liberty, and as a rule it was kept in check by a strong desire for order, and a great respect for the past.

The cautious and thoughtful liberalism of Scotland has frequently and justly been ascribed to the training given by Presbyterianism in self-government and equal representation. In the eighteenth century such training was scarcely given within the Established Church. Wesley tells how he found to his surprise that, in rural Scotland, wealth was held to be an essential qualification for the eldership in parish churches. Sessions so chosen showed a leniency towards the sins of the rich. 'I perceive,' writes a *Journeyer through Scotland* in 1726, 'the poor only suffer by Church censures, for a piece of money will save a man here from the stool of repentance as much as in England.' It was very different with the Seceders. When Ebenezer Erskine opposed a forced settlement at Burntisland, the noble patron excluded him, in retaliation, from an invitation to dinner, saying, 'Mr Erskine, you are none of us to-day.' 'Sir,' he replied, 'you do me great honour; it gives me the truest pleasure that in this we are agreed; for I scorn to be one of those who dare to oppress the Christian people, and to rob them of their just privileges.' It is said that, among the early adherents of the Secession, there was only one man of title, Sir Robert Pringle of Torwoodlee. The cause of liberty had in that generation few advocates among the Scottish aristocracy. Those who were accustomed to deference and influence, on the ground of their birth or wealth, saw nothing to attract them in the Secession Church. Yet it was not among the ignorant and degraded that the Erskines found a response, but among those whose sturdy intelligence rebelled against territorial influence, and who had it in their hearts to lead an independent life. It was much to lay hold of such elements, out of which political partisanship and social revolution have often developed —to show men that liberty and equality were of more importance in religion than in any other department of life, to train them in the exercise of freedom, and at the same time to teach them that, within the Church, they must refrain from 'peddling in politics.' It must be ascribed mainly to the Erskines that secular ideas of liberty were kept in subordination to religious law. Hill Burton, with that insight which justifies his place as a true historian, and more than atones for his supercilious treatment of Presbyterian affairs, has pointed out that the Seceders, from the outset, avoided politics in their Church courts, and strove to confine themselves to spiritual matters. This disposition, which was the direct outcome of the views of the Erskines, showed itself in both branches of the Secession, and kept them in line with the general sentiment of the country. There was not the faintest resemblance between the normal Seceder and Matthew Arnold's 'political dissenter.' Yet the Secession Church steadily trained men in the exercise of their own rights, and in sympathy with the claims of others for liberty.

By their strict adherence to the Presbyterian polity and creed, the Erskines differentiated the nonconformity of Scotland from the nonconformity of England. In England, the gap between Congregational and Episcopalian methods and ideas has a width which the most sanguine prophet of Church union finds it difficult to bridge. The Wesleys, too, though even more reluctant than the Erskines to sever connection with the Established Church, formed a Church differing from Episcopacy in doctrine, worship and government. But the Erskines took a plan which led to no such divergence. Except by giving a somewhat more popular bent to Church arrangements, their descendants, while claiming a liberty to change, have refrained from exercising that liberty, and have adhered for 167 years to their appeal to the 'first free, faithful, and reforming Assembly of the Church of Scotland.' The present unity and solidarity of religious conviction and feeling in Scotland, the fact that in countless parishes, where political differences are keen, the whole population is Presbyterian, the absence of strife upon such matters as the teaching of religion in public schools, the impending union between the Church of the Secession and the Church of the Disruption, and the widely spread consciousness, in the Established and non - Established Churches, of historical identity and common interests—these are the historical vindication of the principles of the Erskines. Their ideas of State-religion could no more be transplanted into the twentieth century than could the ideas of Carstares or Robertson, but their ideas of the liberty of the Church and of liberty of conscience are now generally accepted in Scotland, even by men who never read a word of their writings, and who have been trained by sectarian teachers to speak of them as rigid and schismatical dogmatists. The opinion which marked them off from all their contemporaries—it was a principle rather than an opinion—that national religion has a definite meaning and worth, wholly apart from the particular Church which has parliamentary privileges, is an opinion, a principle, likely to regulate the future of Christian nations. It would be preposterous to suggest that they designed or foresaw such developments. They did not pitch their utterances upon a prophetic key. But steady and sure instincts led them to recognise the difference between blundering Church courts and the true Church of the country, to push their claims no further than their own consciences required, to look backwards as well as forwards when they seceded, and to regulate every step of their procedure by those Church laws which they believed to have divine authority. Protestants have rarely been successful in riding the marches steadily, between Church authority and individual liberty, and when they have succeeded, even partially, it has been through a sane refusal to abandon conviction in obedience to logic, and a willingness to modify their theories by their sentiments. At a time when Protestant State Churches are claiming absolute freedom, and are declaring that, without freedom, Establishment would have little worth, it seems needless to vindicate men who protested against the surrender by the Church of her inherent liberty, and who, when they were forcibly silenced, courageously took a place of freedom, with little of the extravagance that attends dissent as its shadow.

Apart from their special opinions and actions, the Erskines were brave men. It has been well said that, if they had lived in the previous century, they would have been preachers on the hills or sufferers in the Grassmarket. Not impulsively, but after careful thought, and with no conceivable motive of a selfish kind, they took an untrodden path, knowing that they would imperil their homes, lose the associates of their youth and manhood, be misrepresented and maligned. Their actual sufferings and sorrows were different from their expectations. They were wounded in the house of their friends. But when the wounds cut deepest they neither swerved nor repined. In old age they were unmoved by the violent reproaches of their former followers, as they had been, in their maturity, by the threats and sneers of the Assembly.

The explanation is clear. Religion was everything to them. Their lives were impregnated by an intense conscience, and devoted to God without reserve. Their antagonists called their piety pretentious, but utterly failed to convict them of pretence. Ralph may be justly charged with over-keenness in controversy, and Ebenezer with rigour and severity in judgment. Both of them were violent in denunciation of prevailing evils, and occasionally lost sense of proportion and propriety. Yet these are the faults of men who are absolutely sincere in their beliefs, and supremely concerned for the welfare of the Church. They are faults from which no man, who has exercised a permanent influence upon the religion of his country, has been completely free.   The Secession of the Erskines would have been a passing commotion, if their great natural ability, the justice of their contention and the prudence of their plans, had not been supported by a deep and devout religion.   It was their unaffected goodness, and their love for the living Christ, that impressed their nearest friends, and secured for them what is better than fame.